I0412187

June 2014

DIPLOMATIC SECURITY

Overseas Facilities May Face Greater Risks Due to Gaps in Security-Related Activities, Standards, and Policies

GAO-14-655

GAO Highlights

Highlights of GAO-14-655, a report to congressional committees

DIPLOMATIC SECURITY

Overseas Facilities May Face Greater Risks Due to Gaps in Security-Related Activities, Standards, and Policies

Why GAO Did This Study

U.S. policy can call for U.S. personnel to be posted to high-threat, high-risk posts overseas. To maintain a presence in these locations, State has often relied on older, acquired (purchased or leased), and temporary work facilities that do not meet the same security standards as more recently constructed permanent facilities.

GAO was asked to review how State assures the security of these work facilities. GAO evaluated (1) how State manages risks at work facilities overseas; (2) the adequacy of State's physical security standards for these facilities; (3) State's processes to address vulnerabilities when older, acquired, and temporary overseas facilities do not meet physical security standards; and (4) the extent to which State's activities to manage risks to its overseas work facilities align with State's risk management policy and with risk management best practices. GAO reviewed U.S. laws and State's policies, procedures, and standards for risk management and physical security. GAO reviewed facilities at a judgmental sample of 10 higher-threat, higher-risk, geographically dispersed, overseas posts and interviewed officials from State and other agencies in Washington, D.C., and at 16 overseas posts, including the 10 posts at which GAO reviewed facilities.

What GAO Recommends

GAO is making 13 recommendations for State to address gaps in its security-related activities, standards, and policies (detailed on the following page). State generally agreed with GAO's recommendations.

View GAO-14-655. For more information, contact Michael J. Courts at (202) 512-8980 or courtsm@gao.gov.

What GAO Found

To manage risks at its overseas work facilities, the Department of State (State) tracks information about each facility, assesses threat levels at posts, develops security standards to meet threats facing different types of facilities overseas, identifies vulnerabilities, and sets risk-based construction priorities. For example, State assesses six types of threats, such as terrorism, and assigns threat levels, which correspond to physical security standards at each overseas post. However, GAO found several inconsistencies in terminology used to categorize properties and within the property inventory database used to track them, raising questions about the reliability of the data. For example, GAO identified a facility categorized as a warehouse that included offices and therefore should have been subject to more stringent standards. Gaps in categorization and tracking of facilities could hamper the proper implementation of physical security standards.

Although State has established physical security standards for most types of overseas facilities, GAO identified some facility types for which standards were lacking or unclear, instances in which the standards were not updated in a timely manner, and inconsistencies within the standards. The following are examples:

- It is unclear what standards apply to some types of facilities.
- In some instances, updating standards took more than 8 years.
- One set of standards requires anti-ram perimeter walls at medium- and higher-threat posts; another required them only at higher-threat posts.

Furthermore, GAO found that State lacks a process for reassessing standards against evolving threats and risks. GAO identified several posts that put security measures in place that exceed the standards because the standards did not adequately address emerging threats and risks. Without adequate and up-to-date standards, post officials rely on an ad hoc process to establish security measures rather than systematically drawing upon collective subject-matter expertise.

Although State takes steps to mitigate vulnerabilities to older, acquired, and temporary work facilities, its waivers and exceptions process has weaknesses. When posts cannot meet security standards for a given facility, the posts must submit requests for waivers and exceptions, which identify steps the post will take to mitigate vulnerabilities. However, GAO found neither posts nor headquarters systematically tracks the waivers and exceptions and that State has no process to re-evaluate waivers and exceptions when the threat or risk changes. Furthermore, posts do not always request required waivers and exceptions and do not always take required mitigation steps. With such deficiencies, State cannot be assured it has all the information needed to mitigate facility vulnerabilities and that mitigation measures have been implemented.

GAO found that State has not fully developed and implemented a risk management policy for overseas facilities. Furthermore, State's risk management activities do not operate as a continuous process or continually incorporate new information. State does not use all available information when establishing threat levels at posts, such as when posts find it necessary to implement measures that exceed security standards. State also lacks processes to re-evaluate the risk to interim and temporary facilities that have been in use longer than anticipated. Without a fully developed risk management policy, State may lack the information needed to make the best security decisions concerning personnel and facilities.

_____ United States Government Accountability Office

What GAO Recommends

Specifically, GAO is recommending that the Secretary of State:

1. Define the conditions when a warehouse should be categorized as an office facility and meet appropriate security standards.

2. Harmonize the terminology State uses to categorize facilities in its security standards and property databases.

3. Establish a routine process for validating the accuracy of the data in State's property database.

4. Establish a routine process for validating the accuracy of the data in State's risk matrix.

5. Identify and eliminate inconsistencies between and within State's physical security guidance.

6. Develop physical security standards for facilities not currently covered by existing standards.

7. Clarify existing flexibilities to ensure that security and life-safety updates to the security standards are updated through an expedited review process.

8. Develop a process to routinely review all security standards to determine if the standards adequately address evolving threats and risks.

9. Develop a policy for the use of interim and temporary facilities that includes definitions for such facilities, time frames for use, and a routine process for reassessing the interim or temporary designation.

10. Automate waivers and exceptions documentation, and ensure that headquarters and post officials have ready access to the documentation.

11. Routinely ensure that necessary waivers and exceptions are in place for all work facilities at posts overseas.

12. Develop a process to ensure that mitigating steps agreed to in granting waivers and exceptions have been implemented.

13. Develop a risk management policy and procedures for ensuring the physical security of diplomatic facilities, including roles and responsibilities of all stakeholders and a routine feedback process that continually incorporates new information.

To manage risk to overseas work facilities, State conducts a range of ongoing activities, including the setting of security standards. However, GAO identified a number of problems with these activities. Moreover, GAO found that State lacked a fully developed risk management policy to coordinate these activities (see figure).

State's Key Risk Management Activities and Decisions Concerning Facility Security and Problems Identified by GAO

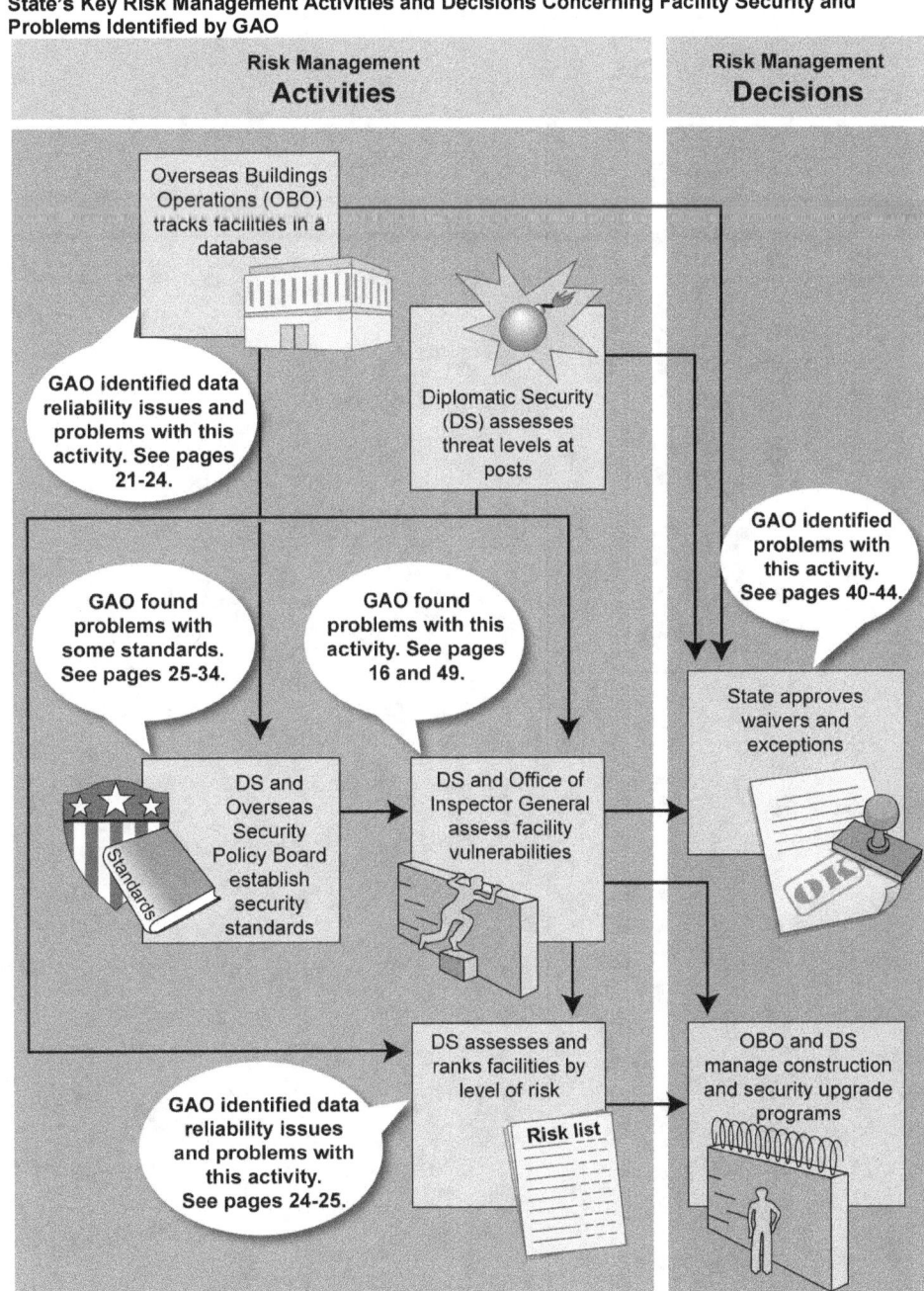

Source: GAO (analysis); Department of State (data). | GAO-14-655

This is the public version of a Sensitive but Unclassified report by the same title.

Contents

Figures

Abbreviations

ARB	Accountability Review Board
DS	Bureau of Diplomatic Security
FAH	Foreign Affairs Handbook
FAM	Foreign Affairs Manual
M/PRI	Office of Management Policy, Rightsizing, and Innovation
OBO	Bureau of Overseas Buildings Operations
OIG	Office of Inspector General
OSPB	Overseas Security Policy Board
RSO	Regional Security Officer
SECCA	Secure Embassy Construction and Counterterrorism Act of 1999
State	Department of State
USAID	U.S. Agency for International Development

GAO

U.S. GOVERNMENT ACCOUNTABILITY OFFICE

441 G St. N.W.
Washington, DC 20548

June 25, 2014

The Honorable Robert Menendez
Chairman
The Honorable Bob Corker
Ranking Member
Committee on Foreign Relations
United States Senate

The Honorable Edward R. Royce
Chairman
The Honorable Eliot L. Engel
Ranking Member
Committee on Foreign Affairs
House of Representatives

Since the 1998 East Africa bombings, U.S. personnel working in diplomatic facilities overseas have faced increasing threats to their safety and security, including numerous attacks in high-risk locations. These threats have been heightened in part due to policy decisions to keep staff in locations that previously would have been deemed too dangerous for U.S. personnel. To establish or maintain a U.S. presence in these and other locations, the Department of State (State) often relies on older, acquired, and temporary diplomatic facilities that do not meet the same security standards as more recently constructed permanent facilities. On September 11, 2012, the acquired facilities at the U.S. Special Mission compound in Benghazi, Libya, came under attack. Tragically, four U.S. officials were killed, including the U.S. Ambassador. From September 2012 through December 2013, 53 attacks against U.S. embassy facilities and personnel occurred, including 4 attacks that resulted in the deaths of U.S. embassy personnel. These attacks raise questions about the security of U.S. diplomatic facilities, particularly those facilities not built to current security standards, such as the facility in Benghazi. In response to the attack, State has begun taking a number of steps to enhance its risk management and security efforts aimed at protecting overseas facilities. For example, shortly after the attacks in Benghazi, State, working with the Department of Defense, sent out Interagency Security Assessment Teams to evaluate the security at 19 higher-threat, higher-risk posts. Those teams made a number of recommendations to improve physical and procedural security at each post, and State has begun to implement them.

GAO-14-655 Diplomatic Facility Security

You asked us to review how State assures the security of older, acquired, and temporary work facilities overseas.[1] We evaluated (1) how State manages risks to work facilities under chief-of-mission authority overseas; (2) the adequacy of State's physical security standards for these work facilities; (3) State's processes to mitigate vulnerabilities when older, acquired, and temporary work facilities overseas do not meet physical security standards; and (4) how State's risk management activities align with its risk management policy and risk management best practices.

To address these objectives, we reviewed U.S. laws; State's physical security policies and procedures as found in memoranda, guidance, the Foreign Affairs Manual (FAM), and Foreign Affairs Handbooks (FAH)—most notably, the Physical Security Handbook and the Overseas Security Policy Board (OSPB) standards; State's Bureau of Diplomatic Security (DS) documentation of overseas posts' physical security surveys, threat and risk ratings, and physical security waivers and exceptions; post-specific documents pertaining to physical security; State's Bureau of Overseas Buildings Operations (OBO) construction and physical security upgrade documentation; U.S. Agency for International Development (USAID) physical security documentation; State and USAID budgetary documents; classified and unclassified Accountability Review Board (ARB) reports resulting from physical security attacks and State's documents evaluating their response to ARB recommendations; past GAO, State Office of Inspector General (OIG), and Congressional Research Service reports; and reports by Congressional committees and independent panels. We also interviewed officials in Washington, D.C., from DS; OBO; State's Office of Management, Policy, Rightsizing, and Innovation (M/PRI); and USAID about risk management and physical security policies and standards and their implementation.

---

[1] For the purposes of this report, the term "work facilities" refers to nonresidential and nonrecreational facilities, such as offices or warehouses. By "older work facilities," we mean facilities that State constructed prior to June 1991, when State adopted new security-related construction standards. Approximately two-thirds of all embassy and consulate compounds were constructed prior to June 1991. Our review included these older work facilities but excluded newer facilities that State constructed after issuing the June 1991 standards. In 2013, State's Office of Inspector General issued a report on the extent to which newer facilities met security standards. See Department of State Office of Inspector General, *Audit of Department of State Compliance with Physical and Procedural Security Standards at Selected High Threat Level Posts*, AUD-SI-13-32 (Washington, D.C.: June 2013).

We evaluated the reliability of OBO's facility data in State's property database, as well as the data DS uses to assess risk. Our concerns about these data are discussed in our findings. We evaluated the consistency of physical security standards within the FAM and FAH and the timeliness of updates to those policies. We also asked State, USAID, and other agency officials at 16 posts overseas in-person and by video-conference a standard set of questions regarding the implementation of physical security policies and procedures. We traveled to 12 posts and conducted work focused on 4 other posts by teleconference. Our judgmental sample included nine countries in three of State's geographic regions—Africa, the Near East, and South and Central Asia. In addition to ensuring geographic coverage, we selected posts that had relatively high DS-established threat and risk ratings and had facilities that were generally older, acquired, or temporary. For security reasons, we are not naming the specific posts we visited for this review. At 10 posts we visited, we evaluated the compliance of all work facilities at the post—a combined total of over 40 different offices and warehouses—against the existing physical security standards. In general, the facilities in our sample were not comparable to those on recently constructed embassy or consulate compounds, which were constructed to meet current security standards. Our findings from these posts are not generalizable to all posts. We assessed DS's risk management policies against best practices identified by GAO as well as federal standards for internal control.[2]

We conducted this performance audit from March 2013 to June 2014 in accordance with generally accepted government auditing standards. Those standards require that we plan and perform the audit to obtain sufficient, appropriate evidence to provide a reasonable basis for our findings and conclusions based on our audit objectives. We believe that the evidence obtained provides a reasonable basis for our findings and conclusions based on our audit objectives.

The original version of this report is a restricted report and was issued on June 5, 2014, copies of which are available for official use only.[3] This

---

[2]GAO, *Risk Management: A GAO Analysts' Guide*, v. 2.2 (Washington, D.C.: July 2005), and *Standards for Internal Control in the Federal Government*, GAO/AIMD-00-21.3.1 (Washington, D.C.: November 1999).

[3]GAO, *Diplomatic Security: Overseas Facilities May Face Greater Risks Due to Gaps in Security-Related Activities, Standards, and Policies* (Washington, D.C.: June 5, 2014).

public version of the original report does not contain certain information that State regarded as Sensitive but Unclassified and requested that we remove. We provided State a draft copy of this public report for sensitivity review, and State agreed that we had appropriately removed all Sensitive but Unclassified information.

Background

Attacks against U.S. Diplomatic Missions Resulted in Legal and Policy Changes

U.S. diplomatic missions have faced numerous attacks in recent years, resulting in legal and policy changes. According to DS, between January 1998 and December 2013, there were 336 attacks against U.S. personnel and facilities.[4] Several of those attacks resulted in the deaths of U.S. personnel, destruction of U.S. facilities, or both including recent attacks in Benghazi, Libya, in September 2012, and in Ankara, Turkey, and Herat, Afghanistan, in 2013.

Several of the deadly attacks against U.S. personnel and facilities overseas have led to new legislation, independent reviews with corresponding recommendations, or both (see fig. 1 for a timeline of selected attacks and related laws and reports). For example, the Omnibus Diplomatic Security and Antiterrorism Act of 1986,[5] which followed the attacks against the U.S. Embassy in Beirut, Lebanon, in 1983, established many of the policies and procedures discussed in this report, including the formation of the Bureau of Diplomatic Security and setting of its responsibility for post security and protective functions abroad. The Secure Embassy Construction and Counterterrorism Act of 1999 (SECCA),[6] which followed the Africa embassy bombings of 1998, set requirements for colocation of all U.S. government personnel at an overseas diplomatic post (except those under the command of an area military commander) and for a 100-foot perimeter setback for all new U.S. diplomatic facilities.

---

[4]This total excludes over 209 indirect fire attacks in Iraq between 2008 and 2012.

[5]Pub. L. No. 99-399 (codified at 22 U.S.C. § 4801 et seq).

[6]Pub. L. No. 106-113, div B, § 1000(A)(7) (incorporating by reference H.R. 3427 of the 106th Congress and codified at 22 U.S.C. § 4865).

GAO-14-655 Diplomatic Facility Security

Figure 1: Timeline of Selected Attacks against U.S. Missions and Related Laws and Reports, 1986-2013

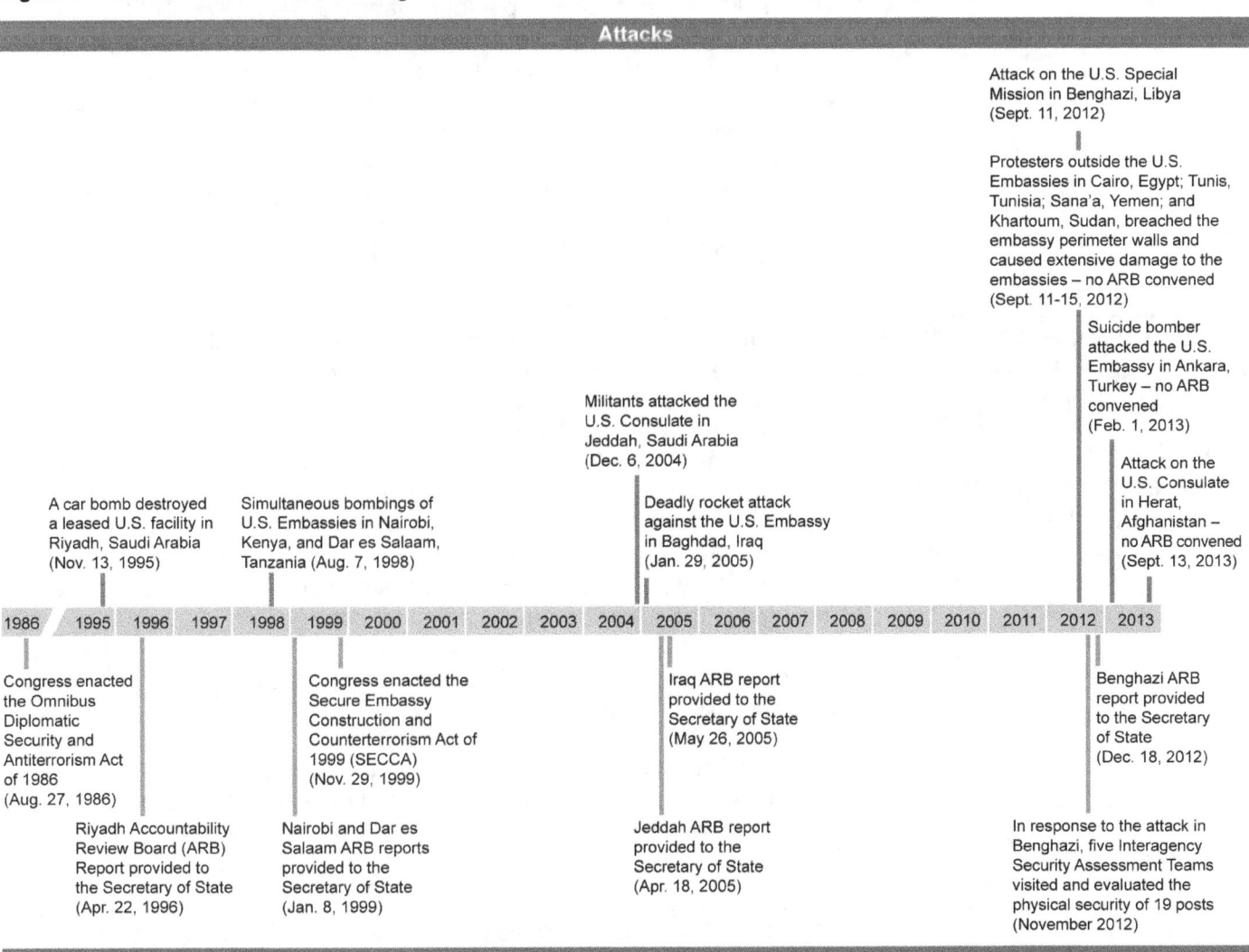

Source: GAO (analysis); Department of State and open source (data). | GAO-14-655

Note: ARBs are convened to report on the circumstances of attacks and make recommendations following serious injury, loss of life, or significant destruction of property involving U.S. diplomatic mission and personnel abroad.

In addition, since 1998, 12 attacks resulted in the formation of ARBs, the most recent of which formed in response to the September 11, 2012, attacks against the U.S. Special Mission in Benghazi, Libya. ARBs, required by law, are convened by the Secretary of State in cases of serious injury, loss of life, or significant destruction of property involving U.S. diplomatic missions or personnel abroad.[7] The review boards are responsible for reporting their findings about the circumstances of the attack and making recommendations. The Benghazi ARB report, for example, made 29 policy recommendations, including several concerning how State manages risk at high-threat, high-risk posts. State concurred with all of them. Furthermore, two of State's actions resulting from that ARB led to additional reports that included more recommendations, and according to State officials, State concurred with most of the recommendations from those additional two reports.

State Bureaus and Offices Responsible for Physical Security of U.S. Diplomatic Facilities Abroad, Numbers of Facilities, and Funding for Physical Security of Facilities

The Omnibus Diplomatic Security and Antiterrorism Act of 1986 requires that the Secretary of State (in consultation with the heads of other federal agencies) develop and implement policies and programs, including funding levels and standards, to provide for the security of U.S. government diplomatic operations abroad.[8] State's policies are detailed in the FAM[9] and corresponding FAH; these include the Overseas Security Policy Board (OSPB) standards[10] and the Physical Security Handbook[11] specifications to guide implementation of the standards. In June 1991, State adopted new security-related construction standards, which are included in the FAH and have continued to evolve.[12]

Responsibility for diplomatic facility security falls principally on two State bureaus, DS and OBO.

- DS is responsible for, among other things, establishing and operating security and protective procedures at posts, developing and implementing posts' physical security programs, and chairing the

---

[7]See 22 U.S.C. § 4831. The Secretary of State was not required to convene ARBs for incidents occurring in Afghanistan or Iraq between fiscal years 2006 and 2009.

[8]Pub. L. No. 99-399, § 103 as amended (codified at 22 U.S.C. § 4802).

[9]12 FAM 300.

[10]12 FAH-6.

[11]12 FAH-5.

[12]Buildings that were occupied or had completed at least 35 percent of their construction prior to June 1991 are considered existing office buildings. In many cases, existing office buildings are only required to meet security standards to the maximum extent feasible.

interagency process that sets security standards. In addition, at posts, it is the DS agents known as Regional Security Officers (RSOs), including Deputy RSOs and Assistant RSOs, that are responsible for protection of personnel and property, documenting threats and facility vulnerabilities, and identifying possible mitigation efforts to address those vulnerabilities, among other duties.

- OBO is responsible for the design, construction, acquisition, maintenance, and sale of U.S. government diplomatic property abroad, establishing construction programs—including those for most facility and security-related construction—and providing direction and guidance on construction matters abroad to State regional bureaus and other agencies.

State's overseas posts also play a role in setting post-specific security measures and funding some physical security upgrades, with approval from DS. In addition, M/PRI manages State's implementation of ARB recommendations and State's Bureau of Administration coordinates State's clearance process regarding updates to the FAM and FAH. (See fig. 2 for an organizational chart of the key State offices responsible for physical security.) USAID maintains its own Office of Security, which is responsible for the physical security of its facilities and coordinating with DS.[13]

---

[13]Other agencies operating overseas may also have security offices, but none of them operating under chief-of-mission authority, aside from the Department of Defense and the intelligence community, maintain their own facilities outside of DS's responsibility.

Figure 2: Department of State Organizational Chart of Key Offices with Physical Security and Related Administrative Responsibilities

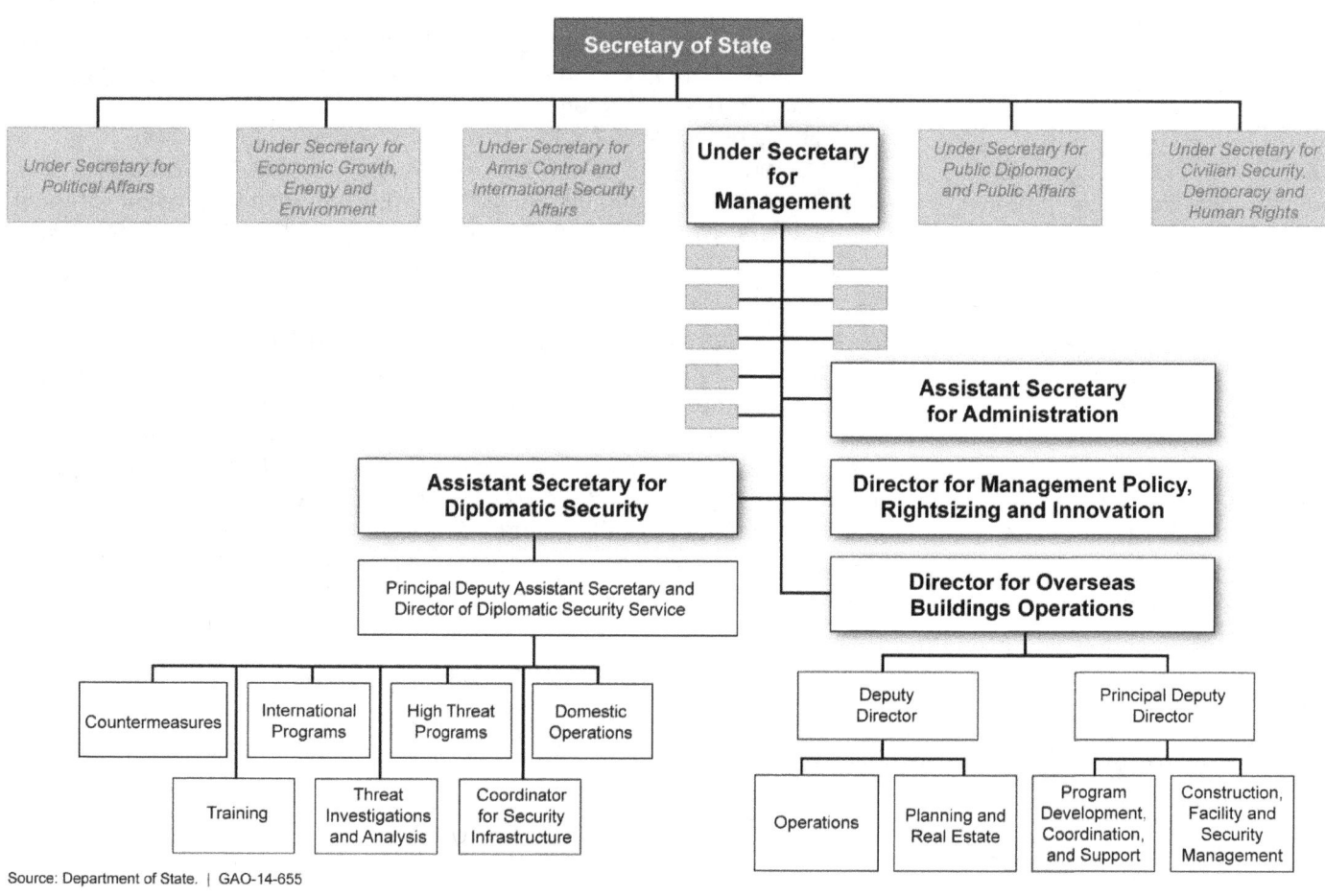

Source: Department of State. | GAO-14-655

According to OBO, State maintains approximately 1,600 work facilities, which includes offices and warehouses,[14] at 275 diplomatic posts—embassies, consulates, and missions—worldwide under chief-of-mission authority. A significant number of State's embassies and consulates predate the June 1991 construction standards. State constructed approximately 475 of the work facilities, including over 120 new embassy and consulate compounds and annex facilities built to the newer construction standards. In addition, State acquired—purchased or leased—over 1,125 work facilities. According to State officials, State has a limited number of temporary work facilities, mostly in high-risk locations such as Afghanistan.[15] In addition, USAID maintains over 25 independently leased facilities.

In fiscal years 2009 through 2014, State allotted about $8.3 billion directly to construction of new secure facilities and physical security upgrades to existing and acquired facilities (see table 1). While DS has a few small programs to provide physical security upgrades to facilities abroad, most of the allotted funds were managed by OBO. DS and OBO have detailed the conditions under which each bureau is responsible for funding security construction and upgrades. In general, OBO is responsible for constructing new facilities and funding upgrades to owned facilities and leased office facilities, while DS is responsible for funding physical

---

[14]There are six types of work facilities: (1) embassy and consulate compounds—the primary diplomatic compound at posts; (2) sole occupant facilities and compounds—office facilities or compounds outside of the embassy or consulate compound that are only occupied by U.S. agencies; (3) tenant of commercial office space—office facilities in a commercial office building located outside the embassy or consulate compound that are also occupied by non-U.S. government agencies; (4) public office facilities—facilities that are used for public functions, such as libraries and cultural centers, that are located in commercial office buildings; (5) Voice of America relay stations—facilities that rebroadcast Voice of America broadcasts in shortwave and medium wave to audiences around the world; and (6) unclassified warehouses—facilities used exclusively for the storage of supplies and materials for U.S. facilities at posts.

[15]For the purposes of this report and according to State's Office of the Legal Advisor and OBO, temporary facilities refer to those facilities that can be disassembled and moved, such as trailers. According to State officials, OBO uses this definition for temporary facilities for appropriations purposes. Nevertheless, State has also used the terms "temporary" and "interim" to refer to those facilities that it did not intend to permanently occupy, such as those at the Special Mission in Benghazi, Libya. According to officials, if State sets up a facility in a location but has not decided to establish a permanent presence in the location, it refers to it as a "temporary" facility. If State establishes a permanent presence in a location with the intent to remain only until a new embassy compound or new consulate compound can be built, it is referred to as an "interim" facility.

security upgrades to leased residential facilities. State runs other programs, such as OBO's major rehabilitation program and DS's technical field support efforts, which may include physical security upgrades; however, we did not include funding from these sources in table 1. USAID has also allotted about $0.03 billion to directly support physical security upgrades.

Table 1: Dedicated Allotments for Physical Security at Diplomatic Facilities, Fiscal Years 2009-2014

In millions of nominal dollars

	FY2009	FY2010	FY2011	FY2012	FY2013	FY2014	Total[a]
Department of State (State) Bureau of Overseas Building Operations Worldwide Security Upgrades[b]	$1,868.0	$847.3	$793.4	$808.0	$1,907.1	$1,864.0	$8,087.8
State's Bureau of Diplomatic Security physical security	$21.4	$21.8	$17.8	$23.1	$17.3	$85.2	$186.6
USAID physical security upgrades	$3.3	$4.1	$5.3	$4.2	$7.4	$6.6	$30.9
Total dedicated allotments	**$1892.7**	**$873.2**	**$816.5**	**$835.3**	**$1931.8**	**$1995.9**	**$8305.3**

Legend: FY = fiscal year.

Source: GAO analysis of data from State and the U.S. Agency for International Development (USAID). | GAO-14-655

[a]Rows may not sum to totals due to rounding.

[b]Worldwide Security Upgrades includes allotments for construction of new secure facilities and physical security upgrades to existing and acquired facilities.

State Conducts a Range of Activities to Manage Risks to Overseas Facilities; However, Gaps Exist in Categorizing Facilities and Ensuring Data Reliability

To manage risk to overseas facilities under chief-of-mission authority, State conducts a range of ongoing activities (see fig. 3), and after the September 2012 attacks, it took additional steps to improve risk management activities. Nonetheless, we found problems with facility categorization and data reliability that may affect State's ability to accurately track facilities and rank them by the risks they face.

GAO-14-655 Diplomatic Facility Security

Figure 3: State's Key Risk Management Activities and Decisions Concerning Facility Security

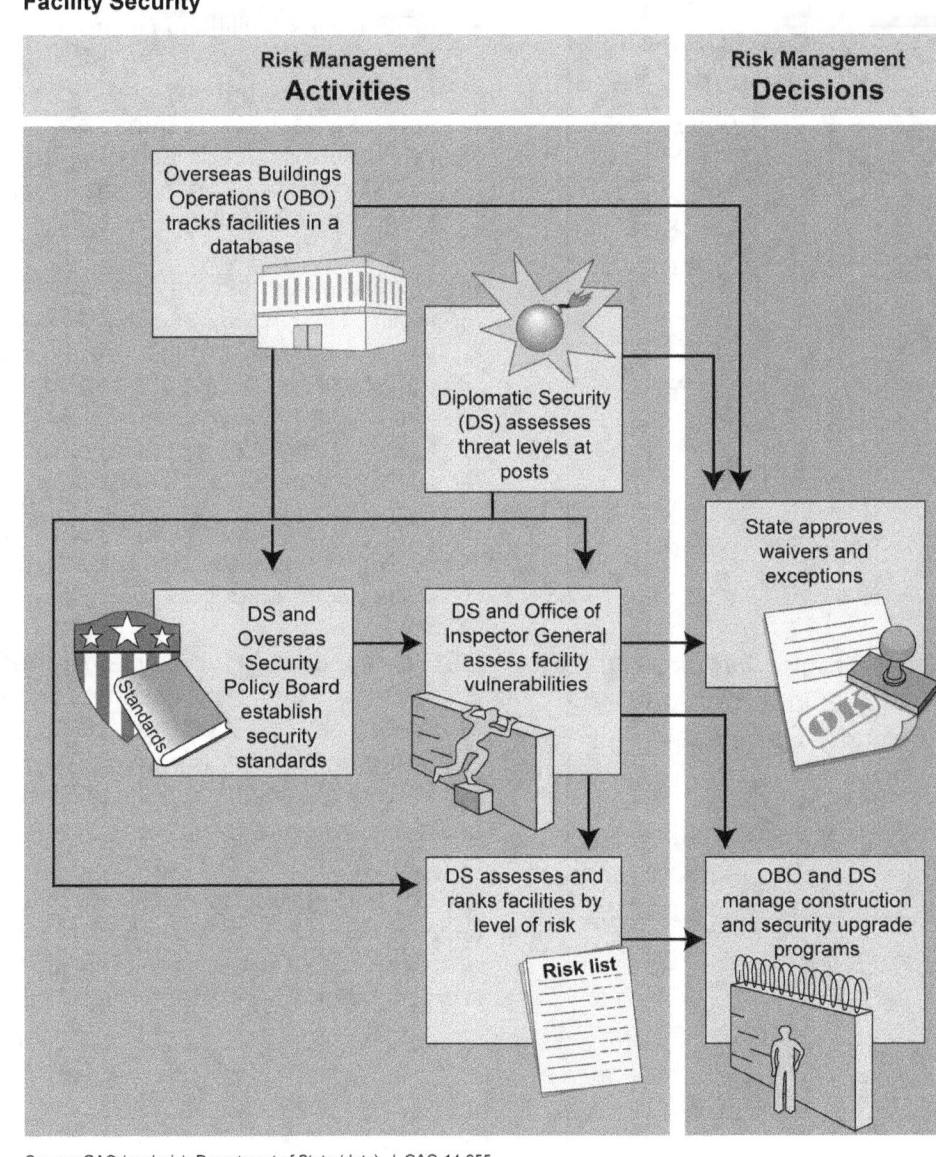

Source: GAO (analysis); Department of State (data). | GAO-14-655

State Manages Risk to Overseas Facilities through Several Activities and Has Recently Taken Steps to Improve These Activities

State conducts several key activities to manage risk to overseas facilities:

- OBO tracks facilities in a property inventory database, and OBO and other bureaus rely on the information in this database to inform a number of security-related decisions.
- DS uses security-related questionnaires completed by officials at each post to assess and determine threat levels at each overseas post.
- Working through an interagency group, DS establishes security standards for facilities overseas, which vary depending on the threat levels at each post.
- Guided by the security standards, officials at posts periodically assess facilities to identify security deficiencies or vulnerabilities.
- DS analyzes information from OBO's property inventory database, the threat assessments, and the vulnerability assessments to assess the risk faced by overseas facilities. DS then ranks facilities by the level of risk each facility faces to help OBO prioritize embassy and consulate construction plans.

In addition to these ongoing activities to manage risk, State has taken steps to implement recommendations resulting from several post-Benghazi reports such as the ARB.

OBO Tracks Overseas Facilities in a Property Inventory Database

OBO is responsible for maintaining records on all diplomatic residential and work facilities overseas in its property inventory database (hereafter referred to as OBO's property database).[16] According to OBO officials, OBO and other State bureaus rely on this database for data on over 1,600 work facilities.[17] OBO's property database includes data for facilities State or USAID owns or leases, including facilities located outside embassy and consulate compounds—such as office spaces and warehouses—and facilities outside both the work and residential categories—such as recreational facilities. OBO's property database does not include host-government facilities where U.S. agencies may operate, such as laboratories supported by the Centers for Disease Control.

---

[16]Diplomatic facilities include those used by State and USAID. OBO houses USAID's property records in its property database.

[17]This database contains data on over 20,000 facilities, including ancillary facilities on embassy and consulate compounds, such as tool sheds, pool houses, generator rooms, gazebos, and other facilities, such as residences.

According to OBO officials, OBO has undertaken several efforts since early 2012 to improve the quality of the information in its property database. For example, OBO hired additional staff to review the reliability of the data in the system, and these staff identified outdated records and missing information. In addition, in response to the Benghazi ARB report, OBO requested that all posts provide (1) a list of all facilities located off compound and (2) the number of desk positions at each facility. OBO intended to use this information to ensure that OBO's property database contained records on all off-compound work facilities. According to OBO officials, the updated information from posts had been entered into its property database as of spring 2013.

DS Assesses Threat Levels at Posts Overseas

DS assesses six types of threats at each overseas post by evaluating the post's security situation and assigning a corresponding threat level,[18] which is used to determine the security standards required for facilities at that post. Published annually by State, the Security Environment Threat List documents each post's threat levels for six threat categories, including political violence, terrorism, residential, and nonresidential crime.[19] Each post is assigned one of four threat levels for each threat category. The levels are as follows:

- *critical:* grave impact on American diplomats;
- *high:* serious impact on American diplomats;
- *medium:* moderate impact on American diplomats; and
- *low:* minor impact on American diplomats.

According to DS officials, the bureau develops the Security Environment Threat List threat levels for each post based on questionnaires filled out by post officials, and the final threat ratings are reviewed and finalized through an iterative process involving officials at overseas posts and in headquarters.

A DS-Led Interagency Board Establishes Physical Security Standards for Diplomatic Work Facilities

DS, in conjunction with the interagency OSPB, reviews and issues uniform guidance on physical security standards for diplomatic work facilities overseas. Chaired by the Assistant Secretary of DS, OSPB includes representatives from approximately 20 U.S. agencies with personnel overseas, including intelligence, foreign affairs, and other

---

[18]For the purposes of this report, "threat" is defined as the likelihood of an event, such as an attack or crime against U.S. personnel or property.

[19]The other two Security Environment Threat List categories are classified.

agencies. State incorporates the OSPB's physical security standards in the FAH[20] for the six types of overseas work facilities, including embassy and consulate compounds.[21] Facilities overseas, whether permanent, interim, or temporary, are required to meet the standards applicable to them.[22] The OSPB standards vary by facility type, date of construction or acquisition, and threat level. If facilities do not meet all applicable standards, posts are required to request waivers to SECCA requirements, exceptions to OSPB standards, or both.

Within State's physical security standards, we identified six categories of key security requirements, to protect overseas work facilities against physical attacks and other dangers: (1) a 100-foot setback from the perimeter wall, (2) anti-climb perimeter walls and "clear zone," (3) anti-ram protection, (4) hardened building exteriors, (5) controlled access to the compound or facility, and (6) a safe space for taking refuge during an attack (see fig. 4 for an illustration of the six categories at a notional embassy).

---

[20]Throughout this report, we use "OSPB standards" to refer to only the physical security standards within 12 FAH-6, which also contains procedural and technical standards.

[21]OSPB incorporated the setback requirement from SECCA into the OSPB standards.

[22]12 FAH-6 H-110 and 12 FAH-6 H-520.

Figure 4: Key Physical Security Standards at a Notional Embassy

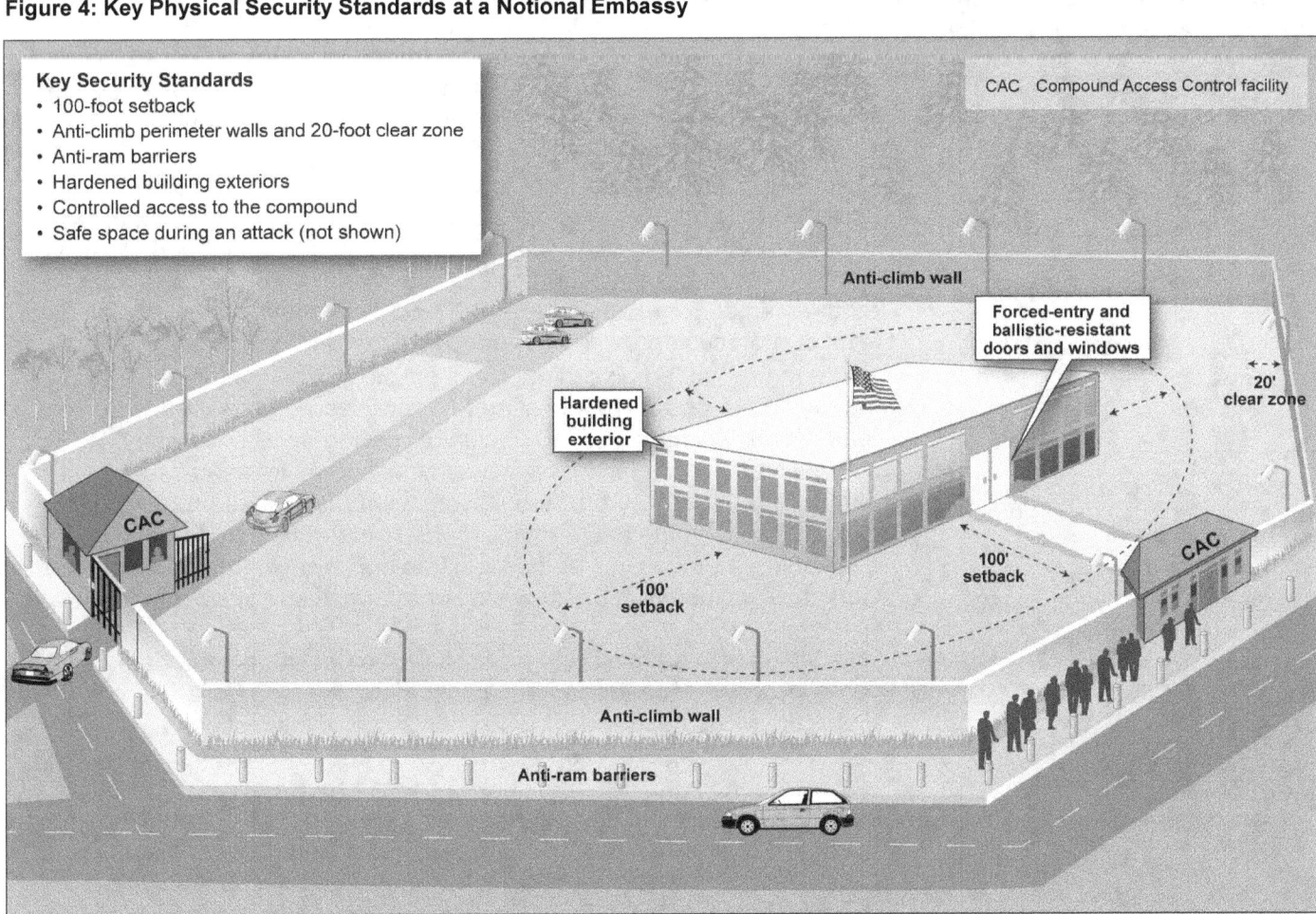

Key Security Standards
- 100-foot setback
- Anti-climb perimeter walls and 20-foot clear zone
- Anti-ram barriers
- Hardened building exteriors
- Controlled access to the compound
- Safe space during an attack (not shown)

CAC   Compound Access Control facility

Anti-climb wall

Forced-entry and ballistic-resistant doors and windows

20' clear zone

Hardened building exterior

100' setback

100' setback

CAC

CAC

Anti-climb wall

Anti-ram barriers

Source: GAO (analysis); Department of State (data); and Nova Development (clip art). | GAO-14-655

In addition to the OSPB standards, State independently developed and continues to update the Physical Security Handbook, also published in the FAH, which provides detailed supporting information, such as construction specifications and diagrams, to help officials understand how to implement and meet the OSPB standards. State has supplemented the physical security standards found in the FAH with guidance found in other sources, such as OBO's construction manuals or guidance sent out to posts.

DS and the OIG Periodically Assess Facility Vulnerabilities

DS and State's OIG periodically assess facility vulnerabilities to identify security deficiencies.[23] For example, RSOs at every post are to inspect the physical security of (1) each work facility at least once every 3 years to identify vulnerabilities and (2) potential properties prior to acquisition.[24] To support these security assessments, DS developed a physical security survey template to guide RSOs in conducting the facility inspections. According to DS officials, during these inspections the RSOs are expected to identify all instances in which a facility does not meet OSPB standards. However, while visiting posts, we learned that not all RSOs know how to determine whether a facility meets certain security requirements. For example, one RSO did not know how to determine the level of protection provided by a forced-entry and ballistic-resistant door.[25] Furthermore, based on our review of physical security surveys for 50 facilities at 14 posts, we identified four facilities with out-of-date surveys and 14 facilities for which DS could not provide us with a survey. DS is currently redesigning the physical security survey templates and automating the survey process, which may address the problems we identified. According to DS officials, RSOs in the field had already evaluated 44 embassies and consulates and a smaller number of other work facility types with the new survey templates as of November 2013.

The OIG is also supposed to inspect each overseas post once every 5 years; however, due to resource constraints, the OIG Office of Inspections has not done so. The OIG Office of Inspections has conducted inspections in an average of 24 countries per year (including all constituent posts within each country) in fiscal years 2010 through 2013. Given their limited resources, according to OIG officials, they have prioritized higher-risk posts. OIG's post inspections cover all aspects of post management, including consular affairs, public diplomacy, and security, among other things. Each inspection team, according to OIG officials, includes one or two security inspectors who evaluate all aspects

---

[23]For the purposes of this report, "vulnerability" is defined as a physical security weakness.

[24]12 FAM 315.2.

[25]Forced-entry and ballistic-resistant doors and windows are given a rating based on how long they are designed to defend against an attack; thus, a 15-minute forced-entry and ballistic-resistant door should provide at least 15 minutes protection from attackers trying to (1) force open a door or window with basic tools or (2) shoot through a door with a military rifle or shotgun.

of a post's security, including compliance with OSPB standards. Following the inspection, the OIG provides a report with all recommendations to the post's management, DS, OBO, and other relevant bureaus which are required to respond to the OIG's recommendations.

DS Assesses and Ranks Facilities According to Levels of Risk to Help OBO Set Construction Priorities

DS combines facility, threat, and vulnerability data to rank the level of risk faced by overseas facilities.[26] This risk matrix forms the basis for OBO's new embassy and consulate construction plans. According to DS officials, to develop the list of facilities ranked in the risk matrix, DS obtains a list of work facilities from OBO. To rank embassy and consulate compounds and off-compound facilities according to the risks they face, DS draws data from its threat and vulnerability assessments—including the threat levels for political violence and terrorism, host-country willingness and capability ratings,[27] facility setback distance, and a facility rating for compliance with security standards. DS's risk matrix also draws staffing data, such as numbers of desk positions and percentages of off-compound desk positions, from OBO's annual colocation study, which enables OBO to collect updated staffing information from posts. The DS risk matrix was developed for OBO to identify facility replacement priorities in accordance with SECCA, which mandated that State submit a report annually from 2000 to 2004 that identified diplomatic facilities that were a priority for replacement or for any major security enhancement because of vulnerability to a terrorist attack.[28] DS has continued this practice and now typically updates the risk matrix annually. OBO uses the risk matrix to develop its Capital Security Construction Program schedule, which identifies the highest priority posts for contract awards over the next 5 years. This schedule takes into consideration the availability of

---

[26]For the purposes of this report, "risk" is defined as the combination of threats, vulnerabilities, and the consequence of loss of personnel and property.

[27]For the purposes of this report, "host-country willingness" refers to the extent to which the government of a host country is willing to protect U.S. government personnel and facilities located within its borders, and the extent to which the host country is responsive to U.S. requests for protective security. For example, host countries may provide military or police support or close roads to vehicular traffic around U.S. facilities to protect U.S. personnel and facilities against threats. "Host-country capability" refers to the extent to which the government of a host country is capable of protecting U.S. government personnel and facilities located within its borders. Capability is based on a number of factors, including the host country's financial resources, infrastructure, and police and military readiness.

[28]See 22 U.S.C. § 4865 note.

land at each post, the feasibility of obtaining construction permits, and other factors.

DS has, on occasion, modified the factors scored in the risk matrix to address the changing risk environment, according to a DS official. For example, in 2010, OBO requested that DS include the percentage of off-compound desk positions as one of the factors used in ranking facilities in the risk matrix. For the most current version, DS split the host-government capability and willingness score into two separate scores to reflect the increased emphasis on these factors following the September 2012 attacks.

State Has Taken Several Actions to Enhance Its Risk Management Activities since the September 2012 Attacks

Since the September 2012 attacks against U.S. facilities overseas, State has taken several actions to better manage risks to work facilities overseas, including (1) conducting interagency facility security assessments, (2) creating the High Threat Programs Directorate in DS, and (3) taking steps to address recommendations from the Benghazi ARB report. In response to the September 2012 attacks against overseas facilities—including facilities in Libya, Sudan, Tunisia, Yemen, and Egypt, among others—State formed several Interagency Security Assessment Teams to assess security vulnerabilities at 19 posts that DS considered to be high-threat and high-risk.[29] Each team was led by a senior DS agent and included a DS physical security expert, and two U.S. military officials. Rather than assess the facilities at the 19 posts against the OSPB standards, the teams assessed all facilities at the 19 posts for any type of security vulnerability—physical or procedural. The Interagency Security Assessment Team process resulted in a report that included a list of recommendations for State, and more specifically, recommendations for DS and OBO to install additional physical security upgrades. For example, the teams recommended that many posts install concertina wire to increase the height of their perimeter walls and further improve anti-climb measures, a security enhancement that exceeds the OSPB standards. According to State officials, State immediately began upgrading the security at 5 of the 19 posts assessed by the Interagency Security Assessment Teams and is using fiscal year 2013 and 2014

---

[29]According to State officials, in developing the list of posts for the Interagency Security Assessment Team process, State focused on three criteria: the extent to which a post complied with physical security standards; the political willingness and capability of the host government to protect U.S. facilities; and posts' terrorism and political violence threat ratings from the Security Environment Threat List.

funds to upgrade security at the other posts. According to State officials, these upgrades resulted in the deferral of planned security projects at other posts.

In addition, State created the new High Threat Programs Directorate within DS to ensure that those posts facing the greatest risk receive additional security-related attention. To determine which posts should fall under the new Directorate, DS developed a high-threat post risk list to rank posts, using many of the same criteria and data points used to rank facilities in the risk matrix that DS provides to OBO. Currently, the High Threat Programs Directorate is responsible for 27 posts in 20 countries and for 2 posts where operations are currently suspended. State plans to conduct annual and as-needed reviews of posts on the high-threat posts risk list, which could change the composition of the list.

Moreover, the Secretary of State convened an ARB following the attacks in Benghazi, and State plans to take action on all of the ARB recommendations. In addition, that ARB made two recommendations that led to the formation of other panels that reported on various aspects of State's security operations.[30] State is also taking action to address most of the recommendations from those two panels' reports.

- *Action taken to address the Benghazi ARB recommendations:* State agreed with all 29 of the ARB recommendations and as of April 2014, according to State officials, has implemented 15 of the recommendations. For example, State developed a method—the Vital Presence Validation Process—by which it can systematically review the "proper balance between acceptable risk and expected outcomes in high-threat, high-risk areas" when beginning, restarting, continuing, modifying, or discontinuing operations at individual posts. According to State officials, this transparent and repeatable process will help State determine the appropriate presence overseas through a documented, systematic, risk-based analysis. To address another recommendation, State developed a new process involving multibureau support cells and checklists to provide an action plan for opening a new post or reopening a post that had closed due to security concerns. State published checklists to support this process

---

[30]Department of State, *Accountability Review Board for Benghazi Attack of September 2012* (Washington, D.C.: Dec. 19, 2012).

in the FAM and,[31] according to State officials, State has already applied the process on at least two occasions.

- *Action taken to address the DS Organization and Management Panel's recommendations:* Based on a Benghazi ARB recommendation, State established a panel to evaluate the organization and management of DS. This panel provided State with its report in May 2013,[32] and State accepted 30 of the 35 recommendations in the report. According to State officials, State has begun taking action to address these recommendations. For example, the panel recommended several organizational changes that State has already implemented, including raising three DS Assistant Director positions to Deputy Assistant Secretary positions. However, State does not plan to implement a recommendation to restructure responsibilities for the new High Threat Programs Directorate. State also does not plan to implement a recommendation concerning the creation of a DS chief of staff. Decisions on the other two recommendations concerning activities by the Bureau of Intelligence and Research are pending until the bureau's vacant assistant secretary position is filled.

- *Action taken to address the Independent Panel on Best Practice's recommendations:* In response to the Benghazi ARB, State also established a panel of outside, independent experts with experience in high-threat, high-risk areas to help DS identify best practices for operating in these environments. The Independent Panel on Best Practices published its report in August 2013,[33] and State plans to implement 38 of its 40 recommendations. State has begun taking action to address these recommendations. For example, State is developing (1) an accountability framework to document institutional and individual accountability and responsibility for security throughout the department and (2) a department-wide risk management policy. However, according to State officials, State has decided not to implement the panel's recommendation that waivers to established security standards only be provided subsequent to the implementation of mitigating measures and State has not decided whether to

---

[31] 2 FAM 423.

[32] Department of State, *Diplomatic Security Organization and Management* (Washington, D.C.: May 2013).

[33] Department of State, *Report of the Independent Panel on Best Practices* (Washington, D.C.: Aug. 29, 2013).

GAO-14-655 Diplomatic Facility Security

implement the recommendation to elevate DS out of the Bureau of Management and create a new under secretary position for DS.

Problems with Categorizing Facilities and Ensuring Data Reliability May Impact State's Tracking and Ranking of Facilities

Although State conducts a range of ongoing activities to manage risk to facilities overseas, we identified facility categorization and data reliability problems that may impact these activities:

- DS and OBO have not defined the conditions that would determine when a warehouse with desk positions should be categorized as an office facility and meet appropriate office physical security standards.
- State uses different facility categories in its physical security standards and property databases.
- OBO's property database and DS's risk matrix have data reliability problems, including missing and inaccurate data.

DS and OBO Do Not Have a Shared Understanding on When to Categorize Warehouses as Office Facilities

DS and OBO have not agreed on a common definition for desk positions for the purpose of categorizing office and warehouse facilities, a decision which may have security and resource implications. According to best practices identified by GAO concerning the implementation of the Government Performance and Results Act of 1993 (GPRA) Modernization Act of 2010,[34] agencies should have a shared understanding of definitions. Desk positions are those that require the use of designated office space, while positions that do not need office space, such as guards, garden staff, and custodial staff, are considered non-desk positions. These designations help OBO determine how much space is needed when planning construction of an embassy or consulate. However, during interviews with both DS and OBO officials in headquarters, we learned that DS and OBO do not agree on when a warehouse with desk positions must meet office standards. According to State officials, as of May 2014, DS and OBO began working together to establish a policy to determine when a warehouse with desk positions should be categorized as an office facility.

According to DS officials, posts are allowed to have some part-time desk positions in warehouses, such as those for warehouse supervisors who need a computer to manage warehouse activities. Such part-time desk positions, occupied for less than 4 hours per day, are permitted in a warehouse without the warehouse having to meet office security

---

[34]See GAO, *Managing for Results: Key Considerations for Implementing Interagency Collaborative Mechanisms*, GAO-12-1022 (Washington, D.C.: September 2012).

standards. However, the DS officials also noted that if a warehouse reached an undefined threshold of part-time desk positions, the warehouse would then have to meet office standards.

OBO officials indicated that they did not agree with DS's decision to allow some part-time desk positions in warehouses without those facilities meeting office standards. In addition, when we reviewed an OBO-developed list of office and warehouse facilities located outside of embassy compounds, we identified a number of warehouses being used as offices. OBO officials stated that these facilities should meet OSPB standards for offices instead of those for warehouses, whether or not they are being occupied part time or full time.

During our site visits, we identified several warehouses with office space. In a January 2013 memorandum to State's Under Secretary for Management, State OIG noted it had identified examples of warehouses being used as office space as well.[35] We followed up on the OIG findings during facility reviews at the posts we visited, through document reviews, and during interviews with officials at posts and in headquarters. During our facility reviews, we identified one warehouse compound that included office facilities with desk positions. The RSO who toured the warehouse compound with us stated that the compound should be required to meet the office security standards, which require more rigorous security requirements. In addition, we visited two warehouses at other posts that contained a number of desk positions with computers. DS and OBO's lack of agreement about when a warehouse with desk positions must meet office standards may hamper the implementation of appropriate physical security upgrades at these facilities.

State Lacks Standard Terminology for Different Facility Categories

As noted above, agencies should have a shared understanding of definitions.[36] However, State uses multiple facility categories for the same facilities, and the inconsistency between DS's and OBO's facility categories may limit DS's ability to adequately identify all relevant work facilities. For example, the OSPB standards include specific facility categories for four different types of facilities that are located off

---

[35]See Department of State, Office of Inspector General, *Review of Overseas Security Policy Board Exceptions and Secure Embassy Construction and Counterterrorism Act of 1999 Waivers*, ISP-I-13-06 (Washington, D.C.: January 2013).

[36]GAO-12-1022.

compound: sole occupant facilities or compounds, tenant of commercial office spaces, public office facilities, and Voice of America relay stations. State officials told us that OBO does not use these facility categories in its property database because OBO's property database was designed to meet Federal Real Property Profile reporting requirements.[37] OBO designates work facilities as an office, a warehouse, or a specific type of work facility, such as a library, workshop, medical office, dispatch office, or other facility to meet these reporting requirements. M/PRI officials stated that as they sought to implement Benghazi ARB recommendations, they became increasingly aware that definitional issues across different State bureaus were a challenge and noted that State is working to correct the issue. OBO started working with M/PRI in April 2014 to create a new management tool in which data from OBO's property database will be combined with other data, such as host-government facilities and staffing data. According to State officials, all bureaus will use this management tool to access property information, which they believe will help support the use of more consistent facility categories. DS and OBO are also developing a pilot program to automatically download property data directly from OBO's property database into a DS system to provide ready access to up-to-date property data, rather than relying on intermittent information sharing.

Because DS and OBO use different terminology for facility categories, the process DS follows when developing the risk matrix has weaknesses. To develop the list of facilities ranked in the risk matrix, DS obtains a list of work facilities from OBO that includes over 1,600 facilities. DS consolidates the list, resulting in approximately 400 compounds and off-compound office facilities.[38] However, the differences between DS's and OBO's facility categories has led DS to develop an ad hoc process for creating the list of facilities ranked in the risk matrix. This process has led to inconsistencies, and has caused DS to exclude facilities from the risk matrix or rank duplicative facilities. For example, the DS official responsible for this process stated that DS has listed each tenant office space in the same facility as separate off-compound facilities for some posts but combined them as one off-compound facility for other posts.

---

[37]See Exec. Order No. 13327 (Feb. 4, 2004).

[38]State consolidates all of the facilities in a compound into one entry in its risk matrix and also ranks the individual off-compound facilities.

Moreover, while reviewing a portion of the risk matrix, we identified several tenant office spaces that DS mistakenly omitted.

OBO's Property Inventory Database and DS's Risk Matrix Have Data Reliability Problems

We identified problems with the data reliability of OBO's property inventory database and DS's risk matrix. Our previous work has found that results-oriented organizations make sure that the data they collect are sufficiently complete, accurate, and consistent to support decision making.[39] Although OBO has undertaken a number of efforts to validate the information in OBO's property database, we identified 9 data entry errors in 65 facility data records at eight of the posts we visited. For instance, records for one post included eight off-compound facilities; however, when visiting the post we learned that three of the eight facilities were located at different posts in the same country and that three of the other facilities were actually residential garages. Without accurate data on overseas facilities, OBO and other bureaus relying on data from OBO's property database may not be in a position to make fully informed risk-related decisions. According to State officials, State recently created a standard list of posts, and OBO has committed to using that list to correct errors in the property database by August 2014, which may address some of these data reliability issues.

In addition, DS is missing data for some of the factors evaluated in the risk matrix, and some of the data are incorrect. For example, DS officials did not enter certain data into the risk matrix, including (1) the number of desk positions for some facilities, (2) the threat-level scores for some facilities, and (3) the setback distance for some facilities. Without these data points, the total score for each of the facilities affected by the missing data could be skewed or incorrect. Furthermore, DS officials entered incorrect information for some of the data points in the risk matrix. For example, we identified several examples of embassy and consulate compounds with incorrect percentages of desk positions located off compound, some of which were overstated. We also identified information for two posts' embassy compounds that was out of date and did not reflect the posts' move into new embassy compounds. Because the overall score for each facility in the risk matrix is based on the data for eight factors, missing or incorrect data for even one factor may skew a facility's overall score in the risk matrix, which could affect the information

---

[39]See GAO, *Executive Guide: Effectively Implementing the Government Performance and Results Act*, GAO/GGD-96-118 (Washington, D.C.: June 1996).

that OBO uses in prioritizing embassy and consulate compound construction plans. Moreover, because much of these data are also used in determining which posts fall under DS's new High Threat Programs Directorate, DS may not have accurate information when determining which posts fall under the new directorate.

State Has Established Physical Security Standards for Most Types of Facilities, but Several Lack Standards, and Some Standards Are Problematic

State has developed security standards for most types of facilities but lacks standards for several of them, and we identified problems with some of the existing standards. Lacking standards for several types of facilities, officials are unable to systematically evaluate the security of all facilities. In addition, State's process for updating physical security standards is not timely. In some instances, State and OSPB have taken over 8 years to update standards, which may leave some facilities more vulnerable in the interim. We also identified inconsistencies within the standards that may lead to confusion and the inconsistent application of security standards at posts. Furthermore, although OSPB is required to review the OSPB standards periodically, State does not systematically re-evaluate the existing security standards against evolving threats and risks.

Although State Has Developed Security Standards for Most Types of Facilities, It Lacks OSPB Standards for Several Others

State has developed security standards for a variety of facilities—such as offices and warehouses—but it has not developed OSPB standards for several other types of facilities. For security reasons, we are not naming the types of facilities in this report. For some of these other types of facilities, State issued guidance on physical security requirements in a May 2011 memorandum. However, these security requirements have not been incorporated into the OSPB standards. As a result, some officials at posts we visited were not aware of the physical security requirements found in the memorandum, and the physical security measures in place for such facilities at several of the posts we visited did not meet the outlined security requirements. Federal internal control standards call for reasonable assurance that assets are safeguarded, in part through identifying and assessing risk.[40] Because State lacks OSPB standards for some facilities, officials are unable to systematically conduct risk assessments for these facilities, and consequently, appropriate security

---

[40]GAO/AIMD-00-21.3.1

measures may not be taken, and the personnel working in or using those facilities may be at a greater risk if their facility should come under attack.

State's Process for Updating Its Physical Security Standards Is Not Always Timely

Updating the FAM or the FAH, which includes the OSPB standards and the Physical Security Handbook, is supposed to take about 60 to 90 days, according to DS officials.[41] However, we identified several examples in which the process for updating security standards in the FAM or the FAH took more than 3 years and some that took significantly longer than that. Federal internal control standards dictate that agencies must have timely communication and information sharing to achieve objectives;[42] therefore, it is essential that agencies update their policies in a timely fashion, particularly when the security of lives, property, and information is at stake. DS manages the process by which the OSPB standards and the Physical Security Handbook are updated. DS officials said that it is supposed to take about 60 days to update the Physical Security Handbook, which requires clearance only within State, and 90 days to update the OSPB standards, which requires approval from other OSPB members. Specifically, it is supposed to take 30 days to draft and obtain approval within DS for an update to the security standards and handbook in the FAH and another 30 days to obtain approval for the draft changes by other relevant stakeholders within State, such as OBO and the Office of the Legal Adviser. If the draft changes include changes to OSPB standards, then it is supposed to take an additional 30 days to obtain approval from OSPB members. After all of the required approvals are obtained for changes to either the FAM or the FAH, DS sends the update to the Bureau of Administration for publishing.

We identified two examples of updates to the OSPB standards and the Physical Security Handbook that took 5 to 8 years to complete the process and 11 updates that are still pending after 3 to 8 years in process. Four of these updates resulted from recommendations by previous ARBs. For example, the 2005 ARB resulting from the attacks on the U.S. Consulate in Jeddah, Saudi Arabia, recommended that State

---

[41]Several factors drive revisions and additions to the OSPB standards and Physical Security Handbook, including the need to (1) update out-of-date information; (2) revise information based on changes to the interpretation of a law, statute, or regulation; and (3) address security recommendations made by ARBs or other independent panels.

[42]GAO/AIMD-00-21.3.1.

and OSPB develop residential security standards to address terrorism threats. The OSPB working group completed a final draft of the standards in April 2009, but OSPB has not yet reviewed the draft standards. DS officials said the draft standards have not been sent to OSPB because other relevant State stakeholders have not yet approved them. Officials further noted that because these draft standards have been stalled in the approval process for 3 years, they may need to be modified to address threats that have been identified in the meantime before going to the OSPB for approval, thus re-starting the review process at the beginning.

DS officials said they face two key challenges in managing updates to the OSPB standards and the Physical Security Handbook that at times cause major delays in the update process—a cumbersome review process and subchapter update requirements.

- *Cumbersome review process.* If a stakeholder suggests a change to the draft standard at any time during the review process, the proposed draft must go through the entire review process again (see fig.5). This requirement becomes more time consuming when someone in the later stages of the review process suggests an edit. In addition, DS officials told us that some stakeholders within State or OSPB member agencies may request additional time for reviewing proposed changes, which further delays the process.

Figure 5: Process for Updating the Foreign Affairs Manual and the Foreign Affairs Handbooks

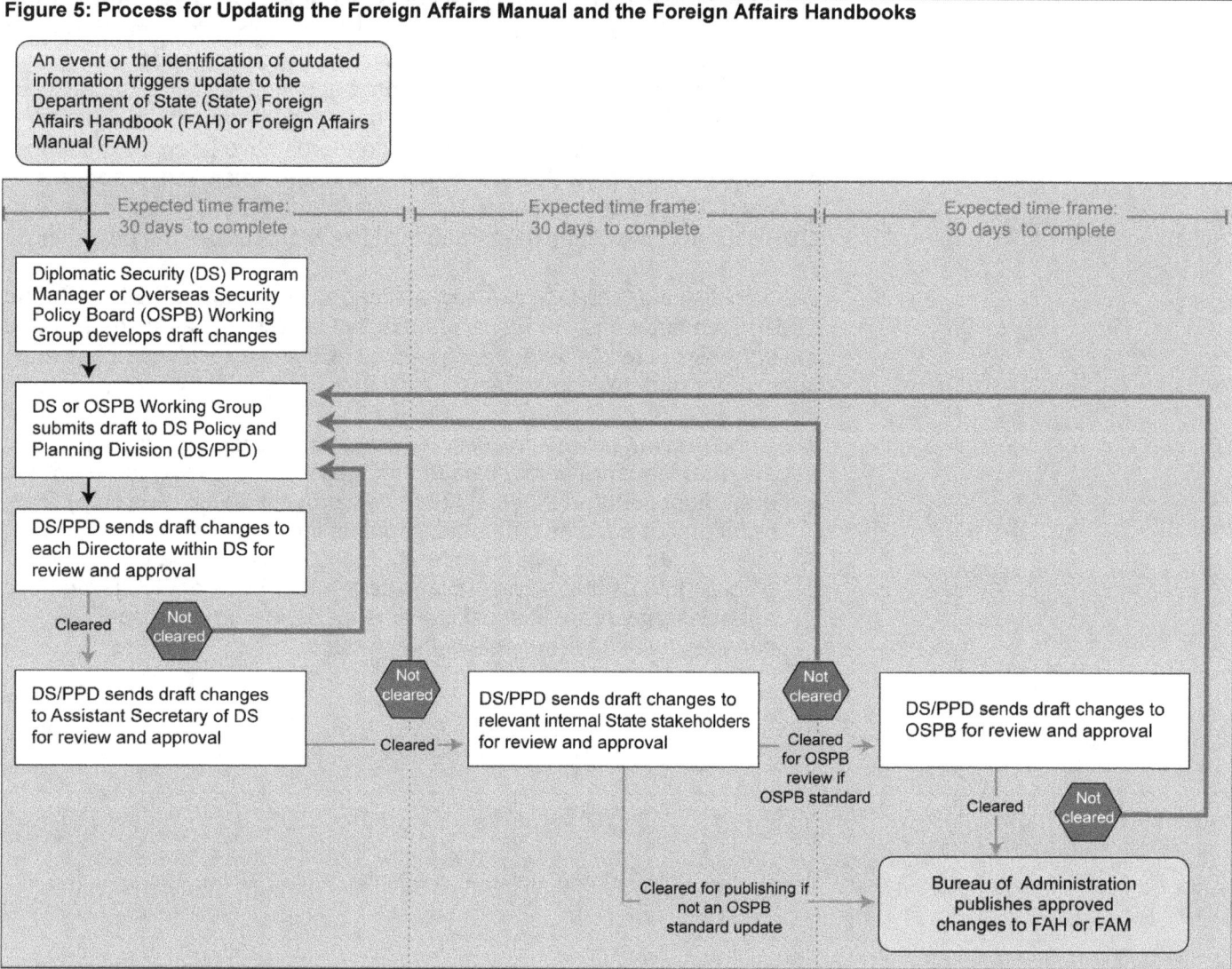

Source: GAO (analysis); Department of State (data). | GAO-14-655

- *FAM and FAH subchapter update requirement.* The FAH requires officials to review and update the entire subchapter when making changes to an existing FAM or FAH subchapter, and there is no specific exception for life safety updates. As a result, when DS needs to make changes to the OSPB standards or the Physical Security Handbook, it must review and update the entire subchapter in which the update is located. As an example of how this requirement delays the process, DS officials told us that draft OSPB standards for compound emergency sanctuaries were begun in 2005 and not completed until 2013.[43] DS finished drafting the standards in 2011, but the standards spent over 2 years in the approval and clearance process because DS and the relevant OSPB working group had to update the entire subchapter, which covers several sensitive security topics. Officials told us that non-State OSPB member agencies did not have any concerns with the compound emergency sanctuary standards, but some members had concerns with the other updates to the subchapter that resulted in additional delays. As noted above, if a stakeholder suggests a change to the draft at any time during the review and approval process, the draft must go through the entire review and approval process again. Because the additional edits occurred during the final stage of the process, each recommended change resulted in a full review of the draft at every level.

According to the FAH, in rare circumstances State's Bureau of Administration will publish specific changes to a section in the FAH or the FAM without requiring a review of the full subchapter.[44] The FAH does not explicitly state when or how such exceptions occur. DS officials said that they were aware of only a few instances in which the Bureau of Administration had granted such an exception. For example, following the Edward Snowden leaks of National Security Agency documents, the Bureau of Administration published changes to technical security requirements without requiring a review of the full subchapter. Officials told us they could not recall any exceptions to the subchapter update requirement on account of critical life safety updates to physical security standards.

Although it may take years for State to update some security standards, we found that State at times took steps to address identified threats in advance of approving updates to the security standards. For example, according to DS officials, DS sometimes works with OBO to quantify the cost of installing certain upgrades for new construction projects to meet draft security standards for which eventual approval is anticipated. If funding is available, OBO will incorporate the upgrades into facilities currently under construction or being planned for construction so that the

---

[43]The 2005 ARB report stemming from the attack in Jeddah, Saudi Arabia, recommended that State consider building a new type of safe space.

[44]2 FAH-1 H-113.1.c.

facilities will meet the draft security standards. For example, OBO included mantraps in new embassy and consulate construction projects following the 2005 attack on the U.S. Consulate in Jeddah, Saudi Arabia, even though OSPB did not approve standards for mantraps until 2010.[45] Furthermore, OBO included the construction of compound emergency sanctuaries in some construction plans before OSPB finalized the relevant standards. Nevertheless, because updates to the OSPB standards and the Physical Security Handbook are not always completed in a timely manner, posts may not have security measures in place to address identified threats.

Inconsistencies within Security-Related Guidance Documents May Lead to Confusion and Inconsistent Application of Some Security Standards

We identified a number of inconsistencies among various security-related guidance documents.[46] Our previous work has found that leading organizations strive to ensure that their core processes efficiently and effectively support mission-related outcomes.[47] To do so, policy standards should be clear and consistent in order to support good decision making.[48] However, we identified about 20 inconsistencies pertaining to physical security standards within State's various security-related guidance documents; such inconsistencies may lead to confusion and the inconsistent application of some security standards. The types of inconsistencies we identified fall into three categories:

- *Inconsistencies between the FAM and the FAH.* For example, in 2010 DS changed the threat categories in the Security Environment Threat List, which impacted security standards, but the corresponding updates to the FAM and the FAH are inconsistent. For example, the

---

[45]Mantraps are anti-climb, fenced-in enclosures intended to prevent unauthorized persons from entering a compound during vehicle inspections and gate operations.

[46]We did not comprehensively review all physical security-related guidance to identify inconsistencies between and within the guidance documents. Rather, we identified the inconsistencies while (1) conducting an analysis of the OSPB standards and the Physical Security Handbook to develop our facility review checklists, (2) reviewing State memoranda concerning physical security requirements, and (3) reviewing a report by the State OIG concerning posts' compliance with security standards. Because it was beyond the scope of this engagement to conduct a systematic review of the consistency of all physical security standards, we cannot generalize our findings to all applicable security standards.

[47]GAO/GGD-96-118.

[48]GAO/AIMD-00-21.3.1.

FAM states that security standards against the terrorism threat are part of the physical security standards.[49] However, there are currently no security standards for the terrorism threat in the OSPB standards within the FAH.

- *Inconsistencies within the FAH between OSPB standards and the Physical Security Handbook.* In some cases, State made an update to either the Physical Security Handbook or the OSPB standards, but not to the corresponding standard in the other part of the FAH. For example, the OSPB standards include requirements for anti-ram perimeter walls at medium- and higher-threat posts, but the Physical Security Handbook used to include this requirement only for higher-threat posts. In addition, DS published physical security specifications for consular agencies in the Physical Security Handbook, but State and OSPB have not approved and incorporated the corresponding standards in the OSPB standards. In other cases, the Physical Security Handbook was outdated. For example, when we visited posts, the Physical Security Handbook contained a physical security standards matrix that did not accurately reflect all the OSPB standards. According to DS officials at headquarters, the matrix has since been updated to address some inconsistencies and is pending final approval.

- *Inconsistencies between the OSPB standards and other policy guidance.* OBO and other State bureaus maintain security-related standards that are not incorporated into the OSPB standards. For example, the Bureau of Consular Affairs requires a consular pass-back booth in the consular section of a controlled access compound facility,[50] but this requirement was never incorporated into the physical security standards. According to DS officials, the draft standard to incorporate this requirement in the Physical Security Handbook is currently pending final approval. Furthermore, the State OIG identified several instances in which the OBO Building and Zoning codes covered additional security requirements not captured in the OSPB standards,[51] and we confirmed their findings.

---

[49]12 FAM 314.

[50]A pass-back booth allows passports to be delivered to the passport applicants so that they do not have to reenter the facility.

[51]See State Office of Inspector General, *Audit of Department of State Compliance with Physical and Procedural Security Standards at Selected High Threat Level Posts*, AUD-SI-13-32 (Washington, D.C.: June 2013).

Inconsistencies among various guidance documents may lead to the inconsistent application of security standards if officials rely on one policy guide over another or are not aware of updated standards. Three different RSOs told us that the physical security standards matrix within the Physical Security Handbook—a list of standards for every type of facility at each threat level—is the primary source they use to evaluate facilities' compliance with physical security standards, because it serves as an easy guide for facilities' physical security requirements. However, as we previously noted, the physical security standards matrix was not up-to-date and did not accurately reflect all the OSPB standards when we visited posts. Hence, these officials may not have applied the appropriate security standards to the facilities at their posts. Some RSOs told us that State updates the OSPB standards and the Physical Security Handbook infrequently and that they learn about updates through DS cables or DS's internal website. However, another two of the RSOs we interviewed did not know about updates made to the security standards in the past few years and therefore had not requested funding for relevant upgrades. For example, they were not aware that State had published standards for compound emergency sanctuaries in the Physical Security Handbook. The inconsistencies in the different security-related guidance documents may lead to confusion and inconsistent application of security standards, leaving some facilities at greater risk because they have not taken all appropriate security measures they are required to address.

State Does Not Systematically Reassess Standards against Evolving Threats and Risks

Although OSPB is required to review its security standards on a regular basis, State does not have a systematic process for evaluating the existing security standards against evolving threats and risks. The 1999 Nairobi and Dar es Salaam ARB report recommended that the U.S. government undertake a long-term strategy for protecting American officials overseas, including the assessment of security requirements to ensure that they meet the new range of global terrorist threats. Furthermore, the FAH requires OSPB to review all the OSPB standards periodically—at least once every 5 years;[52] however, the process by which security standards are updated is either triggered by an event—a change within the organization of State, an annual review to identify out-of-date information, or an attack or other event affecting safety—rather than by a periodic and systematic evaluation of the relevance and

---

[52]12 FAH-6 Exhibit H-014.2.

adequacy of all the standards. Although State has updated the threat categories over the years, many of the physical security standards were developed prior to U.S. diplomatic missions being sustained in or near war zones, where the risks to U.S. personnel and facilities multiply and intensify. Furthermore, State rates numerous posts all over the world as high or critical threat for either political violence or terrorism, but their risk varies greatly due to several factors, including local infrastructure and the host-country government's willingness and capability to provide security for U.S. facilities. Nevertheless, posts with the same threat rating are required to meet the same standards regardless of the risk each post faces. We identified several instances in which State and other officials deemed existing standards inadequate to meet the perceived threats and risks.

- *Interagency Security Assessment Teams recommended security upgrades above current standards:* Following the attacks of September 2012, the teams traveled to a judgmental sample of high-threat, high-risk posts and made recommendations at each post, many of which exceeded the threat standards at the post.
- *Several facilities have security features that exceed requirements:* While reviewing facilities at posts overseas, we identified several examples of facilities that had implemented security measures that exceeded security requirements. For example, at one post rated as having a medium threat for political violence, we found that an agency leasing two floors in an off-compound tenant office facility installed several security measures that exceeded security requirements, such as doors and a guard booth providing 15-minute forced-entry and ballistic-resistant protection—measures only required for tenant office facilities at posts with a critical threat rating for political violence. According to agency officials, they took this action because they did not believe that the OSPB standards addressed the current threats and risks that they faced in country. The RSO and other post officials approved the increased security measures. In addition, we found that posts in certain conflict zones took numerous measures that exceeded critical security standards, such as the construction of overhead cover, higher walls, and bunkers.

Posts may take additional steps on their own or through DS- and OBO-funded upgrades to implement security measures that exceed OSPB standards, because post or headquarters officials believe the standards are inadequate to mitigate against risks faced by some high-threat, high-risk posts. This leaves the establishment of facility-specific security measures up to the professional judgment of post RSOs, an ad hoc process that does not draw on the collective subject-matter expertise of

DS and the interagency OSPB. This current approach to addressing threats and risks not covered by the OSPB standards may leave some high or critical threat posts more vulnerable. In addition, in the absence of standards that address a post's current threats, it may be difficult for post officials to justify funding requests for security measures that go beyond the OSPB standards.

State Mitigates Vulnerabilities for Work Facilities That Do Not Meet Security Standards, but Its Waivers and Exceptions Process Has Weaknesses

State takes steps to mitigate vulnerabilities for older, acquired, and temporary work facilities that do not meet security standards, primarily through a waivers and exceptions process to document vulnerabilities and corresponding mitigation measures; however, the waivers and exceptions process has several weaknesses. All facilities at a post are expected to meet physical security standards, but when facilities do not or cannot meet certain security standards, State mitigates identified vulnerabilities through various construction programs and its waivers and exceptions process. For example, we found that none of the 43 facilities we reviewed at higher-threat, higher-risk posts met all applicable security standards and therefore required waivers, exceptions, or both. However, we identified several weaknesses with the waivers and exceptions process. Specifically, DS does not systematically track waivers and exceptions or re-evaluate them when threats or risks change. In addition, post officials do not always request waivers and exceptions when required, and requests are not always timely or correct. Moreover, in some instances, the mitigating measures a post has agreed to undertake as a condition of a waiver or exception are not fully implemented.

When Facilities Do Not Meet Standards, State Mitigates Security Vulnerabilities through Various Construction Programs and Its Waivers and Exceptions Process

OBO and DS Address Some Security Vulnerabilities through Construction Programs

State addresses identified security vulnerabilities through a number of construction programs, including the Capital Security Construction Program, the Compound Security Program, and the Major Rehabilitation Program. OBO has a threat- and vulnerability-based planning process for its construction projects that includes input from DS's analysis of threats, vulnerabilities, and risk. The risk matrix provided by DS—a ranked list of facilities based on an assessment of the physical security conditions and threat levels at each post—guides OBO's prioritization of new construction projects and compound security projects.

According to OBO documentation, OBO has moved over 30,000 people into safer facilities since 2000 through their various construction programs. The following OBO-managed construction programs address security vulnerabilities:

- *Capital Security Construction Program.* Following the 1998 Africa embassy bombings, State determined that 80 percent of its overseas facilities did not meet security standards and should be replaced. Afterwards, State began a multiyear, multibillion dollar program to replace insecure and aging diplomatic facilities worldwide (see table 2). In 2005, State established the Capital Security Construction Program, through which each agency with an overseas presence contributes funds for construction based on its overseas staffing levels. OBO has constructed 109 new facilities since 1998.

Table 2: Capital Security Construction Program and Related Allotments, Fiscal Years 2009-2014

In millions of nominal dollars

	FY2009	FY2010	FY2011	FY2012	FY2013	FY2014	Total[a]
Capital security cost-sharing	800.5	752.8	705.7	579.2	428.2	1,383.0	4,649.4
Supplemental appropriations[b]	962.8	0	0	0	0.0	0.0	962.8
OBO overseas contingency operations[b]	0	0	0	33.0	1,237.5	250.0	1,521.0
Total	1,763.3	752.8	705.7	612.2	1,665.7	1,633.0	7,133.2

Legend: FY = fiscal year.

Source: GAO analysis of data from the Department of State. | GAO-14-655

[a]Rows may not sum to totals due to rounding.

[b]The Bureau of Overseas Buildings Operations (OBO) used allotments of funds made available pursuant to the Supplemental Appropriations Act of 2009 and from the Overseas Contingency Operations account for fiscal years 2012-2014 to support its capital security cost-sharing program.

- *Compound Security Program.* The Compound Security Program complements the Capital Security Construction Program by providing interim physical security protection to vulnerable facilities until they are replaced, as well as enhancing physical security protection at facilities that will not be replaced by a new embassy or consulate compound. This program funds, among other things, projects to replace forced-entry and ballistic-resistant doors and windows, install emergency exits, and enhance environmental security by safeguarding against chemical, biological, and radiological attacks.

According to OBO officials, major security upgrades at posts cost on average $6 to $10 million but may cost up to $20 million, and since 2005, OBO has completed 53 major security upgrade projects funded by the Compound Security Program. OBO has allotted about $560 million to the program since fiscal year 2009 (see table 3).

Table 3: Compound Security Program Project Allotments, Fiscal Years 2009-2014

In millions of nominal dollars

	Fiscal Years						
	2009	2010	2011	2012	2013	2014	Total
Emergency exit projects	6.0	5.8	5.6	5.0	2.5	0.0	24.9
Environmental security projects	12.5	9.5	9.6	9.0	5.0	8.0	53.6
Forced-entry and ballistic-resistant door and window replacement projects	21.0	16.5	16.6	16.1	23.6	19.1	112.9
Major upgrade projects	43.4	48.2	40.6	38.7	47.4	67.0	285.3
Minor upgrade projects	4.6	4.0	6.3	7.2	3.5	0.0	25.6
Residential upgrade projects	6.2	2.0	1.5	1.0	0.5	1.0	12.2
Soft targets projects[a]	5.0	6.5	5.0	4.0	2.0	4.1	26.6
Other	6.0	2.0	2.5	4.0	0.8	1.8	17.1
Total allotments	**$104.7**	**$94.5**	**$87.7**	**$85.0**	**$85.3**	**$101.0**	**$558.2**

Source: GAO analysis of data from Department of State. | GAO-14-655

[a]Funding for soft targets projects supports security upgrades for overseas recreational facilities, American schools, and other facilities where Americans may gather.

- *Major Rehabilitation Program.* This program provides for renovations, rehabilitations, expansions, or upgrades to systems and space for residential or work facilities that can no longer be physically or economically maintained by routine, preventive, and unscheduled repair activities. In addition, these projects are undertaken when new construction is not scheduled under the Capital Security Construction Program. Although the program is not focused on security upgrades, according to OBO officials, OBO strives to bring facilities up to current security requirements during major rehabilitation projects. State allotted approximately $243 million from fiscal years 2009 to 2014 for major rehabilitation.

DS also provides funding for some physical security upgrades to facilities abroad. Congress appropriates funds for DS through the Worldwide

Security Protection account.[53] DS uses some of the funding to cover emergency upgrades to address emerging vulnerabilities or for upgrades to facilities that will not be addressed by OBO. This is primarily the case in conflict zones such as Afghanistan, Iraq, and Pakistan, but also applies to some other high-threat, high-risk locations. For example, DS used some funding for physical security upgrades to install higher walls in at one post and barricades at another. In addition, officials said that DS funded projects in several countries under the new High Threat Programs Directorate in fiscal year 2013 that cost approximately $2 million and included upgrades for drop-arm barriers to protect against vehicle intrusions and other physical security measures.

When Security Vulnerabilities Are Identified, a Post Must Obtain Waivers or Exceptions That Define Agreed-Upon Mitigation Steps

Diplomatic work facilities are required to meet two sets of physical security standards, SECCA requirements and OSPB standards;[54] however, when facilities do not or cannot meet all of the standards, post officials are required to request waivers to SECCA requirements, exceptions to OSPB standards, or both. SECCA requires that any site selected for a new U.S. embassy or consulate constructed after November 1999 accommodate the colocation all U.S. government personnel (except those under the command of an area military commander), and that any new U.S. diplomatic facility be located at least 100 feet from the perimeter wall. If State or other agencies acquire additional office space off compound, they are required to obtain a colocation waiver prior to occupancy of that facility. Furthermore, if a new facility does not meet the 100 foot setback requirement, the post must apply for a setback waiver. The Secretary of State may waive the SECCA requirements if the Secretary determines that security considerations permit and it is in the national interest of the United States.[55] The FAM notes that the flexibility for State to grant waivers was provided by Congress with the expectation that waivers would be infrequent.[56] According to the FAH, a post must request an exception for a new office construction project or a facility acquired after June 1991 if it does not fully comply with an applicable OSPB standard. Similarly, a post must

---

[53]Worldwide Security Protection funding supports numerous security programs, including a worldwide guard force protecting overseas diplomatic missions and residences.

[54]See 22 U.S.C. § 4865 and 12 FAH-5 H-211.

[55]See 22 U.S.C. § 4865(a).

[56]12 FAM 315.1.

request an exception for an existing office building if the building does not or cannot fully comply with physical security standards following an upgrade project.[57] A waiver or exception request typically includes a description of mitigation steps planned or taken by the post to address identified vulnerabilities. For example, if an acquired facility does not meet blast resistance construction standards for walls, doors, and windows, the post may install additional anti-ram structures outside the perimeter wall to provide additional setback.[58]

The development of waiver and exception requests involves a collaborative drafting and multilevel review process. According to DS officials, the requests are drafted through a collaborative process, with DS officials in headquarters helping the RSO or the tenant agency write the request to ensure that it complies with department policy and appropriately articulates mitigation steps planned or taken by the post to address vulnerabilities. In addition, each waiver or exception request must pass through several layers of review at the post and within State. The Assistant Secretary of DS serves as the final reviewer for all OSPB exception requests and any SECCA waiver requests for facilities other than an embassy or consulate building. The Secretary of State must approve all SECCA waiver requests for embassy and consulate buildings.[59] DS officials said the types of mitigation steps taken in each situation depend on the collective knowledge of the RSO and other DS staff working to mitigate a risk. In addition, the types of mitigation steps possible at individual posts depend on the availability of materials in country, shipping constraints, and host-government policies.

---

[57]12 FAH-5 H-211.

[58]According to State officials, some types of physical security upgrades may be subject to the approval of the host city or nation.

[59]According to 12 FAM 315.1, the Secretary delegated the authority for waiver approvals for embassies or consulates that do not substantially occupy a building—such as an office located in a large commercial office—to the Assistant Secretary of DS.

Many Overseas Work Facilities Do Not Meet the Most Rigorous Security Standards Set for Newly Constructed or Newly Acquired Facilities

Many older, acquired, and temporary work facilities at U.S. posts overseas do not meet SECCA requirements and OSPB standards for newly constructed or newly acquired facilities.

- Since newer facilities are expected to meet more rigorous physical security standards and most existing facilities are not new, most facilities may not meet these standards. Some embassy and consulate compounds are newly constructed and expected to meet most physical security standards. However, a significant number were constructed or acquired prior to June 1991 and are only required to meet many of the OSPB standards to the maximum extent feasible or practicable.[60]
- We found that a substantial portion of the approximately 1,245 office facilities overseas do not meet SECCA requirements and OSPB standards and had requested waivers, exceptions, or both.[61] According to DS documentation, State has processed over 400 setback waivers for various types of office facilities and about 300 colocation waivers for off-compound office facilities, in accordance with SECCA.[62] In addition, DS has processed about 280 OSPB exceptions packages for work facilities—and each exceptions package may include requests for multiple OSPB exceptions for one facility.
- DS rated about a quarter of office facilities as substantially noncompliant with security standards. When DS completed the most recent version of its risk matrix, it evaluated compliance with OSPB standards for approximately 400 office compounds and facilities—including both facilities on embassy and consulate compounds and off-compound office facilities. According to DS documentation, about a quarter of its facilities worldwide received a low facility-compliance score, indicating that they did not substantially meet current OSPB standards for new facilities. However, as noted above, we found that some of the data DS used to establish its ratings for the facilities we visited were missing or inaccurate, and therefore determined that

---

[60]12 FAM 311.2.

[61]SECCA applies to office facilities constructed or acquired after November 1999. State did not provide sufficient information on the 1,245 office facilities to determine how many of them were constructed or acquired after 1999.

[62]The SECCA requirements only apply to office facilities and do not apply to warehouses. See 12 FAM 313.c(6).

DS's scores provide a broad indication of facility vulnerability rather than a precise estimate.

Waivers and Exceptions Are Not Systematically Tracked, Requested, or Reviewed, and Requests Are Not Always Timely, Correct, or Fully Implemented

DS Does Not Systematically Track or Re-evaluate Waivers and Exceptions

As noted above, post officials are required to request waivers to SECCA requirements and exceptions to OSPB standards when facilities do not or cannot meet security standards. Federal internal control standards require the maintenance of complete and accurate documentation and effective use of information technology.[63] However, we identified several weaknesses with the waivers and exceptions process, including tracking problems and missing waivers and exceptions. First, DS is not adequately tracking waivers and exceptions to the security standards. In January 2013, the State OIG reported that DS does not adequately track waivers and exceptions. DS does not maintain a database with waiver and exception documentation, but rather maintains a list of waivers and exceptions in a spreadsheet. When we reviewed DS's tracking spreadsheet, we identified several problems.[64] For example, we found nine instances in which a line item in the tracking spreadsheet contained inaccurate information about the type of approved waivers or exceptions for a facility. In addition, headquarters and post officials we met with could not always find waiver and exception documentation or were unaware of previously approved waivers and exceptions, even though DS officials stated that copies of approved waivers and exceptions are kept both at DS headquarters and at posts. For example, an official at one post told us that the post had two waivers on file that DS officials in headquarters were unable to locate. In addition, officials at three posts were either unaware of certain previously approved waivers and exceptions or could not find the documentation for them.

---

[63]GAO/AIMD-00-21.3.1.

[64]We could only assess the accuracy of the information in the spreadsheet for the 14 posts for which we received approved waiver and exception packages.

We also found that DS did not re-evaluate previously granted waivers and exceptions to security standards for individual facilities when the level of threat or risk changed. For example, the political violence threat rating was low for one post when it obtained approval for exceptions for one facility, but the threat rating has since increased to high. Nevertheless, post and DS officials have not re-evaluated these exceptions. In addition, an agency at one post recently requested and obtained a colocation waiver and exceptions to utilize hotel rooms as office space. There are already two other agencies using the same hotel as office space. The addition of more people at one facility represents an increased risk to this facility, because it becomes a more visible and attractive target. Nonetheless, post and DS officials did not re-evaluate the previously granted waivers and exceptions based on the increased risk.

DS Does Not Systematically Request Waivers and Exceptions

Many of the facilities we reviewed at higher-threat, higher-risk posts[65] did not meet applicable security standards and did not have required waivers and exceptions. We reviewed 43 facilities at 10 higher-threat, higher-risk posts for compliance with applicable security standards—including existing, newly acquired, and a few newly constructed work facilities. While the level of noncompliance varied, all of the facilities are required to have approved waivers, exceptions, or both.

Furthermore, we found that posts we visited did not always request waivers and exceptions when required. Based on our review of 43 facilities, we identified 3 facilities for which the post did not request a required SECCA waiver and 18 facilities missing approved OSPB exceptions (see table 4). For example, DS did not have appropriate waivers on file for 2 of the 8 tenant commercial office spaces we reviewed that did not meet SECCA's colocation or setback requirements. In addition, DS did not have appropriate OSPB exceptions on file for 3 of the 20 embassy or consulate compound facilities we reviewed that did not meet the requirements for hardened building exteriors. Similarly, State OIG identified 4 out of 27 posts that did not submit appropriate waivers or exceptions. To address this problem, State OIG recommended that DS

---

[65]We defined "higher-threat, higher-risk" posts as the 50 posts that DS rated as being the highest-risk on its high-threat posts list. DS used this list to determine the 27 posts that fall under DS's new High Threat Programs Directorate. We purposefully included posts in our scope that were not included under the new directorate but were still among the top 50 higher-threat, higher-risk posts. Of the 10 posts we visited where we also conducted facility reviews, half fell under the High Threat Programs Directorate.

institute an annual certification process in which the Chief of Mission at each post would be required to certify that the post either meets all security standards or that all appropriate waivers and exceptions have been obtained. However, DS officials stated that DS has begun piloting an alternative solution to the recommendation to include a similar certification requirement of the waivers and exceptions as part of its new online physical security survey process. When this solution is fully implemented, posts will be required to verify that all relevant waivers and exceptions have been obtained when RSOs at posts fill out the physical security survey once every 3 years.

Table 4: Extent to Which Posts Obtained Required Waivers and Exceptions for the 43 Facilities GAO Reviewed

Facility type	Number of facilities reviewed	Facilities requiring waivers	Facilities missing waivers	Facilities requiring exceptions	Facilities missing exceptions
Embassy and consulate compound facilities	20	4	1	9	9
Sole occupant facilities and compounds	4	1	0	1	0
Tenant commercial office spaces	8	8	2	2	0
Unclassified warehouses	11	N/A	N/A	9	9
Total	**43**	**13**	**3**	**21**	**18**

Source: GAO. | GAO-14-655

Notes: SECCA does not require posts to obtain setback or colocation waivers for warehouses.

Certain Waivers and Exceptions Were Not Requested in a Timely Manner, Contained Inaccuracies, or Were Not Fully Implemented

We identified additional weaknesses with the 32 waivers and exceptions packages we reviewed,[66] including (1) requests for waivers and exceptions that were filed after the facility was already occupied, (2) incorrect waivers or exceptions on file, and (3) conditions outlined in the approved waiver or exception request that were not always implemented (see table 5). Federal internal control standards require the proper execution of management directives.[67] We obtained these 32 approved

---

[66]We requested all the waivers and exceptions for the 10 posts we visited and for the four posts for which we interviewed RSOs by video conference. Two of the posts did not have waivers or exceptions on file. Because we conducted facility reviews at the posts we visited and discussed security vulnerabilities with RSOs at the four other posts, we were able to review the waiver and exception documents we obtained against other documentation from State and our facility reviews to identify incorrect waivers or exceptions on file, instances in which conditions in the waiver or exception had not been implemented, and other issues discussed in the report. Each waiver and exception package may include one or multiple waivers, exceptions, or both.

[67]GAO/AIMD-00-21.3.1.

waiver and exception packages for 12 of the 14 posts we either visited or for which we interviewed officials by video teleconference.

Table 5: Waivers and Exceptions Packages GAO Reviewed That Were Untimely, Inaccurate, or Not Fully Implemented

Facility type	Number of waivers and exceptions packages	Number of untimely waivers/ exceptions	Number of incorrect waivers/ exceptions on file	Number of waivers/ exceptions not fully implemented	Total number of waivers/ exceptions with problems
Embassy and consulate compound facilities	14	4	3	2	9
Sole occupant facilities and compounds	7	3	0	0	3
Tenant commercial office spaces	11	1	1	1	3
Unclassified warehouses	0	0	0	0	0
Total	**32**	**8**	**4**	**3**	**15**

Source: GAO. | GAO-14-655

Notes: SECCA does not require posts to obtain setback or colocation waivers for warehouses. We reviewed 32 waivers and exceptions packages. Each package may include one or multiple waivers, exceptions, or both.

In our review of these documents, we identified the following problems:

- *Facilities occupied prior to receiving waivers or exceptions.* We identified eight instances in which post officials occupied a facility prior to submitting a required waiver or exception request. For example, officials at one post occupied a temporary facility for over a year and a half before the post obtained a setback waiver.
- *Incorrect waivers or exceptions on file.* We identified four instances in which the waivers or exceptions on file did not cover the facility currently in use or post obtained incomplete or inappropriate waivers or exceptions. For example, one post obtained an approval for a colocation waiver and OSPB exceptions for a temporary medical facility that was located on a residential compound. The proposed medical facility was a one-story safe haven container that provided 60-minute forced-entry, ballistic-resistant protection. When visiting the post, however, we learned that the medical facility was no longer located in the safe haven container; rather, the medical facility was now located in a residential building that did not meet any forced-entry, ballistic-resistant standards for office space. The post had not applied for an updated waiver or exceptions for this facility.
- *Conditions outlined in approved waiver or exception not implemented.* We identified three instances in which posts did not implement mitigating steps that were required conditions for their approved

waivers and exceptions. For example, one post obtained a setback waiver and exceptions in July 2010 on the condition that they implement several upgrades. Although some of the upgrades have since been implemented, we identified three upgrades that had not been implemented when we visited the facility, including (1) improving perimeter walls to ensure they measured 9 feet all the way around the compound, (2) reinforcing the perimeter to ensure all walls were anti-ram, and (3) installing shatter-resistant window film on all the windows. Officials stated that it is the responsibility of post officials or tenant agency officials applying for the waiver or exception to ensure that upgrades agreed to as conditions of a waiver or exception are appropriately implemented, and that they do not currently monitor posts' implementation of conditions agreed to in the granted waivers or exceptions.

Because waivers and exceptions are not always requested, timely, accurate, and fully implemented, State cannot be assured that they have all the information they need and are taking all practical steps to ensure the security of work facilities.

State Follows Some Risk Management Principles but Lacks an Adequate Risk Management Policy for the Physical Security of Work Facilities

State follows some risk management principles; however, it lacks an adequate risk management policy for the physical security of its work facilities. Risk management is a strategy that helps policymakers more efficiently and effectively assess risk, allocate resources, and take actions under conditions of uncertainty.[68] While DS outlined some principles for a risk management policy, it did not fully develop and implement the policy. We found that many of the activities DS takes to manage risk are in line with its risk management principles; however, we found that State's risk management activities do not operate as a continuous process and do not continually incorporate new information. For example, we found that State does not use all available information when establishing threat levels. We also found that State's current facility vulnerability assessments are not fully utilized because, among other things, the information reported by posts through a survey template is not always readily available or timely and is not in a form that facilitates automated processing and data analysis. However, State is taking steps to automate and enhance these surveys. In addition, we found examples in which the

---

[68]For example, see GAO, *Homeland Security: Applying Risk Management Principles to Guide Federal Investments*, GAO-07-386T (Washington, D.C.: Feb. 7, 2007).

data informing DS's risk assessments of facilities had changed, but DS lacked processes to re-evaluate the risk to those facilities. We also found that State lacked a process to re-evaluate interim and temporary facilities that have been in use longer than anticipated. Furthermore, in examining State's feedback mechanisms, we found that State did not adequately verify that it had followed through on some risk-management related recommendations.

DS Established Principles for a Risk Management Policy, but the Policy Has Not Been Fully Developed or Implemented

Past GAO work has shown that risk management is a strategy that helps policymakers more efficiently and effectively assess risk, allocate resources, and take actions under conditions of uncertainty.[69] As we stated previously, an effective risk management policy establishes a structured process for making informed choices and trade-offs about how best to use available resources and for monitoring the effects of those choices. Risk management requires a continuous process that includes the assessment of threats, vulnerabilities, and potential consequences, with actions taken to reduce or eliminate one or more of these elements of risk. Risk management should include a feedback loop that continually incorporates new information, such as changing threats or the effect of actions taken to reduce or eliminate identified threats, vulnerabilities, or consequences. Because policymakers have imperfect information for assessing risks, there is a degree of uncertainty in the information used for risk assessments—what the threats are and how likely they are to be realized. As a result, it is inevitable that assumptions and policy judgments, as well as hard data, influence decisions in risk analysis and management. It is important, therefore, that key decision makers understand the underlying assumptions and policy judgments that have been made and how these affect the results of the risk analysis and the resource decisions based on that analysis. An effective risk management policy, by providing a structured, continuous process with a feedback loop that incorporate new information and adjusts to changing conditions, can provide policymakers with better information with which to make risk decisions in an uncertain environment.

To provide a basis for examining efforts for carrying out risk management, in prior work we developed a framework for risk management based on best practices and other criteria. Our risk management framework is

---

[69]GAO-07-386T.

divided into five phases that form a feedback loop: (1) setting strategic goals and objectives and determining constraints; (2) assessing the risks; (3) evaluating alternatives for addressing these risks; (4) selecting the appropriate alternatives; and (5) implementing the alternatives and monitoring the progress made and the results achieved (see fig. 6). The results generated by monitoring in phase 5 feed back into the ongoing process. In addition, because a framework includes integrated and continually updated information flows, internal controls are crucial. These include the policies, procedures, techniques, and mechanisms that enforce management's directives and are used to help ensure that actions are taken to address risk. We used this framework, as well as the *Standards for Internal Control in the Federal Government*,[70] to assess State's risk management principles and activities.

Figure 6: Five Phases of GAO-Developed Risk Management Framework

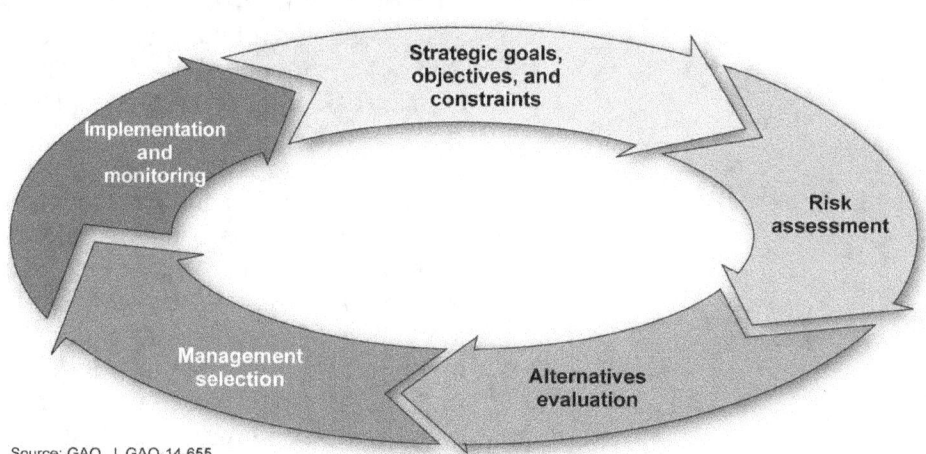

Source: GAO. | GAO-14-655

While DS created a risk management policy statement in 1997, DS has not fully developed and implemented the policy. The one-page policy statement describes six principles: asset identification, threat assessments, vulnerability assessments, risk assessments, risk decisions, and feedback. DS officials noted that a year after the statement was published, its planned implementation was largely overtaken by State's response to the 1998 U.S. embassy bombings in Africa, and that the policy was not fully developed or implemented. For example, DS's risk

---

[70]GAO/AIMD-00-21.3.1.

GAO-14-655 Diplomatic Facility Security

management statement lacks clear roles and responsibilities for all stakeholders and detailed guidance on how to carry out its elements, particularly with regard to implementation and monitoring. Officials further noted that, contrary to what is stated in the policy, there is no formal steering group handling the risk management process. Nevertheless, we also found that many of the activities that DS takes to manage risk align with the DS risk management policy principles and also with our risk management framework, including determining risk by combining the results of asset identification, threat assessments, and vulnerability assessments. Both the Benghazi ARB report [71] and the resulting Report of the Independent Panel on Best Practices[72] recommended that State develop a risk management policy. State has undertaken several efforts to develop a more comprehensive risk management policy. For example, according to State officials, State is applying its recently completed Vital Presence Validation Process to better manage risk when beginning, restarting, continuing, modifying, or discontinuing operations at posts, particularly high-threat, high-risk posts. However, as of February 2014, some of these efforts, including a fully developed risk management policy, remain incomplete.

State's Risk Management Activities Do Not Operate as a Continuous Process and Do Not Continually Incorporate New Information

While many of State's activities align with the DS risk management policy statement, in this report we have identified a number of problems with these activities. Moreover, we found that State's ongoing activities do not operate as a continuous process that incorporates all relevant data and lack a feedback loop that continually incorporates new information (see fig. 7).

---

[71]Department of State, *Accountability Review Board for Benghazi Attack of September 2012.*

[72]Department of State, *Report of the Independent Panel on Best Practices.*

Figure 7: State's Key Risk Management Activities and Decisions Concerning Facility Security and Problems Identified by GAO

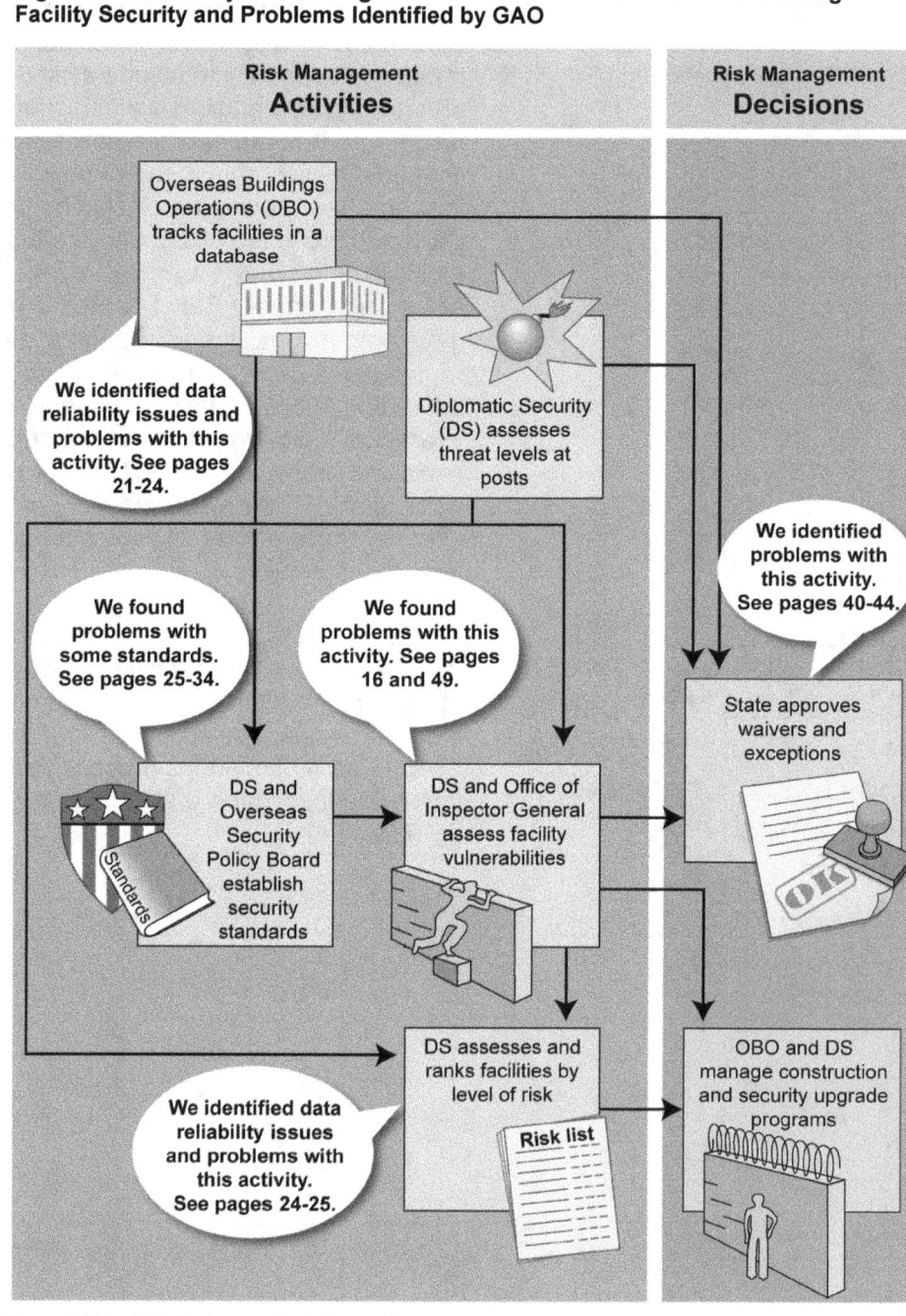

Source: GAO (analysis); Department of State (data). | GAO-14-655

State's Ongoing Risk Management Activities Do Not Operate as a Continuous Process to Incorporate Relevant Data

We found several examples that demonstrate that State's ongoing risk management activities are not fully linked in a continuous process that incorporates all relevant data. For example, we found that DS does not use all available information when establishing threat levels at posts. Specifically, some posts may implement security measures that go above standards, but this type of information is not effectively captured in the triennial facility inspection process to document posts' compliance with OSPB standards, and according to DS officials, does not inform the Security Environment Threat List threat-level decisions.

Furthermore, DS officials noted that the information from the triennial facility inspection process, which is used to identify facility vulnerabilities, is not currently used in a meaningful way because several issues impede DS's ability to collect and adequately use this information. For example, because the survey forms are individual documents housed on an intranet site, DS officials in headquarters cannot easily search through the data from the surveys or conduct comparative analyses of posts' data. In addition, we found that the surveys did not always include all facilities at posts and that headquarters could not always find the most current surveys. DS officials indicated that the new online survey process they are developing will feed certain data into a database, thus improving their ability to analyze and use the survey data. While we have not independently evaluated the online survey forms, DS officials noted that the forms include a checklist for all the current OSPB standards for each of the threat ratings, and RSOs will be required to complete the new survey templates online. In addition, according to officials, DS plans to develop a project management solution that will allow DS officials in headquarters to track and report on the data collected by the completed physical security surveys through an automated system.

Another instance of current information not being fully utilized involves OBO documentation of facility compliance with the physical security standards. According to State's policies, when OBO initiates a major rehabilitation project on a facility constructed prior to June 1991, it must request OSPB exceptions if the planned rehabilitation will not bring the facility into full compliance with current security standards.[73] Furthermore, according to DS officials, when OBO completes a major rehabilitation project on a facility constructed prior to June 1991, the bureau is required

---

[73]12 FAH-5 H-211.

to document with a memorandum what aspects of the facility will still not meet standards after the rehabilitation. However, DS officials told us that no one in DS tracks the OBO memoranda. Without adequately tracking this information, RSOs may not have accurate information to plan mitigation efforts and properly request exceptions to security standards. In addition, as noted above, we also found the DS officials in headquarters do not verify that physical security upgrades included as part of a waiver and exception request are completed.

State's Risk Management Activities Lack a Feedback Loop that Continually Incorporates New Information

We also identified several instances where State's risk management activities did not continually incorporate new information through a feedback loop. For example, as noted above, State does not have a process for evaluating the existing security standards against evolving threats and risks, and we found examples where State officials deemed existing standards inadequate to meet perceived threats and risks. Similarly, DS lacks a process to re-evaluate risk decisions such as the granting of waivers and exceptions when risk factors change. DS quantifies risk to facilities by assessing the number of personnel, threat levels, host-country capability and willingness to support the post, and vulnerabilities. At one post we visited, the consulate initially had a diplomatic presence on one floor of a tenant commercial office space. It received a colocation and setback waiver to occupy that one floor. In subsequent years, as the number of personnel grew, the consulate expanded its office space to include a second floor of the facility. However, according to post officials, there was never a reevaluation of the risk to that facility on the basis of the increased personnel presence, and the post did not request a new waiver until years later when an RSO noticed the discrepancy. Similarly, waiver and exception request packages generally include information about the current Security Environment Threat List levels, but when those levels change—from high to critical, for example—there is, according to DS officials, no process in place to notify post or headquarters to re-evaluate the waivers and exceptions previously granted.

Similarly, DS lacks a process to re-evaluate interim and temporary facilities that have been in use longer than anticipated. When State opens an interim or temporary facility and grants waivers or exceptions, it is with the expectation that the facility will be replaced by another or closed within a certain time frame. There is an explicit acceptance of risk in that decision. However, officials noted that there were a number of facilities that were designated to be used on an interim or temporary basis, but because State lacked a process to re-evaluate these facilities, years later these facilities were still in use without any review of the facility designation and without revisiting of the risk decision. Similarly, the Independent Panel on Best Practices found that State redefined missions, such as Benghazi, as temporary or in other ways that did not require them to meet physical security standards. For example, at some posts, State used containerized housing units and other temporary structures as offices for years though these trailer-like facilities do not meet OSPB standards and were only intended to be used on an interim or temporary basis. State officials stated that they do not systematically review interim and temporary facilities that have been in use longer than anticipated. However, effective risk management practices require a feedback loop that continually incorporates new information, and federal standards for internal controls call for proper execution of management directives.[74]

In addition, we found that State did not adequately verify that it had followed through on the feedback it received through all past risk-management related recommendations. Federal standards for internal controls call for ensuring that the findings of audits and other reviews are promptly resolved. For example, M/PRI maintains documentation to track the implementation of all ARB recommendations. Although we did not assess the reliability of these data, we identified two examples of recommended updates to the OSPB standards that M/PRI's documentation indicated were completed but that our evidence showed had not been completed. During the course of our review, in December 2013, one of these recommendations was completed. Moreover, when we asked DS officials about the status of their efforts to close recommendations resulting from the State OIG's review of their waivers and exceptions process, the officials indicated that they had addressed all of the recommendations. However, in our fieldwork and document reviews, we found that DS had not addressed all of the OIG recommendations.

Conclusions

Ensuring the safety and security of our personnel and facilities at overseas diplomatic posts has never been more challenging or important than it is today. Between September 2012 and December 2013 alone, there were 53 attacks against U.S. diplomatic personnel and facilities overseas. We found that State has taken a number of measures to enhance the security of and manage the risk to its personnel and

---

[74]GAO/AIMD-00-21.3.1.

facilities. For example, State is prioritizing security-related construction using its evaluation of threat and vulnerability levels at posts. In addition, State established a new directorate to provide additional security attention to high-threat, high-risk posts. Furthermore, we found that many of State's risk management activities were consistent with best practices. However, we found a number of problems with State's implementation of some of its activities, rather than with the broader activities themselves. Some of these problems involved the lack of common terminology or the reliability of data that State uses to analyze risk. Others involved the adequacy of its physical security standards. In addition, we found problems with State's handling of its waivers and exceptions process. While each of these problems is a reason for concern, in and of itself, taken as a whole they raise a greater concern that decision makers at State may not have complete and accurate information with which to make risk management decisions. As a result, there is a greater likelihood that security risks to overseas diplomatic facilities will not be adequately addressed—a situation that could have tragic consequences for U.S. government personnel working overseas.

Furthermore, State lacks a cohesive framework or policy to adequately coordinate and control its multifaceted risk management activities. A good risk management policy includes the use of all relevant information and a feedback loop that ensures that changing conditions are assessed and considered by decision makers. Such a policy helps ensure that despite uncertainty, security personnel have a continuous system in place that identifies weaknesses proactively rather than reactively. The lack of such a policy may make State more prone to not considering data needed to make effective risk decisions. While State is developing a risk management framework in response to several recommendations resulting from the attacks in Benghazi, the framework remains incomplete. Unless State implements a risk management policy that addresses the problems we identified with State's current security efforts, State cannot be assured that the most effective security measures are in place at a time when personnel working at U.S. diplomatic facilities are facing ever increasing threats to their safety and security.

Recommendations for Executive Action

To enhance the Department of State's risk management activities, we are making 13 recommendations, which we have categorized into four groups covering (1) consistency and reliability of data; (2) applicability and effectiveness of physical security standards; (3) identification of risks and mitigation of vulnerabilities; and (4) development of risk management policies.

GAO-14-655 Diplomatic Facility Security

To improve the consistency and data reliability of Department of State risk management data, we recommend that the Secretary of State:

1. Direct M/PRI, DS, and OBO to define the conditions when a warehouse should be categorized as an office facility and meet appropriate office physical security standards.

2. Direct M/PRI, DS, and OBO to harmonize the terminology State uses to categorize facilities in State's physical security standards and property databases.

3. Direct OBO to establish a routine process for validating the accuracy of the data in OBO's property database.

4. Direct DS to establish a routine process for validating the accuracy of the data in DS's risk matrix.

5. Direct the Under Secretary for Management to identify and eliminate inconsistencies between and within the FAM, FAH, and other guidance concerning physical security.

To strengthen the applicability and effectiveness of the Department of State's physical security standards, we recommend that the Secretary of State work through DS or, in his capacity as chair, through the OSPB to:

6. Develop physical security standards for facilities not currently covered by existing standards.

7. Clarify existing flexibilities in the FAH to ensure that security and life-safety updates to the OSPB standards and Physical Security Handbook are updated through an expedited review process.

8. Develop a process to routinely review all OSPB standards and the Physical Security Handbook to determine if the standards adequately address evolving threats and risks.

9. Develop a policy for the use of interim and temporary facilities that includes definitions for such facilities, time frames for use, and a routine process for reassessing the interim or temporary designation.

To strengthen the effectiveness of the Department of State's ability to identify risks and mitigate vulnerabilities, we recommend that the Secretary of State:

10. Direct DS to automate its documentation of waivers and exceptions, and ensure that DS officials in headquarters and at each post have ready access to post's waivers and exceptions documentation.

11. Direct DS to routinely ensure that necessary waivers and exceptions are in place for all work facilities at posts overseas.

12. Direct DS to develop a process to ensure that mitigating steps agreed to in granting waivers and exceptions have been implemented.

To strengthen the effectiveness of the Department of State's risk management policies, we recommend that the Secretary of State:

13. Develop a risk management policy and procedures for ensuring the physical security of diplomatic facilities, including roles and responsibilities of all stakeholders and a routine feedback process that continually incorporates new information.

Agency Comments

We provided a draft of this report for review and comment to State and USAID. We received written comments from State, which are reprinted in appendix II. State agreed with 12 of our 13 recommendations and highlighted a number of actions it is taking or plans to take to address the problems that we identified. State noted that it is not in a position to agree or disagree with our recommendation that it develop a policy for the use of interim and temporary facilities because an internal State working group is currently in the process of evaluating this issue. USAID did not provide written comments on the report. We also received technical comments from each agency, which we incorporated throughout our report as appropriate.

We are sending copies of this report to the appropriate congressional committees, the Secretary of State, and Administrator for USAID. In addition, the report is available at no charge on the GAO website at http://www.gao.gov.

If you or your staff have any questions about this report, please contact me at (202) 512-8980 or courtsm@gao.gov. Contact points for our Offices of Congressional Relations and Public Affairs may be found on the last page of this report. GAO staff who made key contributions to this report are listed in appendix III.

Michael J. Courts
Director, International Affairs and Trade

Appendix I: Objectives, Scope, and Methodology

The objectives of our report were to evaluate (1) how the Department of State (State) manages risks to work facilities under chief-of-mission authority overseas; (2) the adequacy of State's physical security standards for these work facilities; (3) State's processes to mitigate vulnerabilities when older, acquired, and temporary work facilities overseas do not meet physical security standards; and (4) how State's risk management activities align with its risk management policy and risk management best practices.

Our scope included older, acquired (purchased or leased), and temporary diplomatic work facilities overseas, such as offices and warehouses built before the June 1991 security-construction standards.[1] For the purposes of travel and review of post-specific documentation, we narrowed our scope to posts determined by State's Bureau of Diplomatic Security (DS) to be high-threat, high-risk posts and which had older, acquired, and temporary diplomatic work facilities. We selected a judgmental sample of 10 posts from the 50 posts rated as the highest-threat, highest-risk. Our selection included posts placed under the new DS High Threat Programs Directorate, as well as those not placed under the new directorate[2] but excluded posts with new embassy compounds. Our sample included posts in nine countries in three of State's geographic regions—Africa, the Near East, and South and Central Asia. We are not naming the specific posts we visited for this review due to security concerns. For these posts, we reviewed the asset, threat, vulnerability, and risk documentation related to the post and its nonresidential facilities and conducted a physical security review of their nonresidential facilities. We conducted interviews at each of these posts with post officials, including DS's

---

[1]The physical security standards address six types of facilities, including: (1) embassy and consulate compounds—the primary diplomatic compound at posts; (2) sole occupant facilities and compounds—office facilities or compounds outside of the embassy or consulate compound that are only occupied by U.S. agencies; (3) tenant of commercial office space—office facilities in a commercial office building located outside the embassy or consulate compound that are also occupied by non-U.S. government agencies; (4) public office facilities—facilities that are used for public functions, such as libraries and cultural centers, that are located in commercial office buildings; (5) Voice of America relay stations—facilities that rebroadcast Voice of America broadcasts in shortwave and medium wave to audiences around the world; and (6) unclassified warehouses—facilities used exclusively for the storage of supplies and materials for U.S. facilities at posts. However, because there were no public office facilities or Voice of America relay stations at the posts we visited, we did not include them in the scope of our engagement.

[2]Of the 10 posts where we conducted facility reviews, half fell under the High Threat Programs Directorate.

Regional Security Officers (RSOs). We also reviewed similar documentation for 4 other high-threat, high-risk posts and interviewed officials about the documentation by video teleconference. In addition to the 14 posts, we traveled to two other posts and conducted interviews with post officials but did not review post-specific documentation or review facilities. Our findings from these posts are not generalizable to all posts. Moreover, our judgmental selection of high-threat, high-risk posts cannot be generalized to other high-threat, high-risk posts.

To provide context and background and address our objectives, we reviewed classified, sensitive-but-unclassified, and unclassified documents, including U.S. laws; State's physical security policies and procedures as found in memoranda, guidance, the Foreign Affairs Manual (FAM), and Foreign Affairs Handbooks (FAH)—most notably, the Physical Security Handbook and the Overseas Security Policy Board (OSPB) standards; DS documentation of anti-U.S. attacks, overseas posts' physical security surveys, threat and risk ratings, and physical security waivers and exceptions; post-specific documents pertaining to physical security; State's Bureau of Overseas Buildings Operations (OBO) facility, construction, and physical security upgrade documentation; U.S. Agency for International Development (USAID) facility and physical security documentation; classified and unclassified Accountability Review Board (ARB) reports resulting from physical security attacks and State's documents evaluating their response to ARB recommendations; past GAO, State Office of Inspector General (OIG), and Congressional Research Service reports; and reports by congressional committees and independent panels. We also interviewed several officials in Washington, D.C., about risk management and physical security policies and standards and their implementation; these officials were from DS; OBO; State's Office of Management Policy, Rightsizing, and Innovation (M/PRI); State's Bureau of Conflict and Stabilization Operations; and State's Bureau of African Affairs; OIG; as well as USAID security officials.

To provide further context and background, we also analyzed State and USAID data of physical security funding allotments, interviewed officials about the data, and found the data to be sufficiently reliable to report at an aggregated level. However, we found that State runs other programs, such as OBO's major rehabilitation program and DS's technical field support efforts, which may include physical security upgrades as part of such projects. We did not include funding from those other State sources in our presentation of the data.

To address how State manages risk to work facilities, we evaluated the
reliability of OBO's facility data in its property database, the timeliness
and tracking of posts' triennial physical security surveys, and the reliability
of the data DS uses to assess risk. To evaluate the reliability of the data
in OBO's property database, OBO provided us with work facility records
pulled from the database between May 2013 and January 2014. We
compared these records to information we collected during discussions
with post officials to identify excess facilities,[3] missing facilities, and
inaccuracies in the data. Although we identified data reliability issues for
some facilities in OBO's property database, as those issues generally
involved the classification or description of facilities, we determined that
the data were sufficiently reliable to describe the approximate number of
U.S. diplomatic work facilities overseas. To review the timeliness of DS's
tracking of posts' triennial physical security surveys, we requested and
obtained most surveys for work facilities at the 14 posts where we
reviewed facility documentation. We reviewed the documentation to
determine whether each survey had been completed in the past 3 years
and reviewed the documents obtained against our list of facilities for each
post to determine if DS provided all the relevant surveys. If DS did not
provide us with a survey we expected, we followed up with DS officials in
headquarters to determine whether or not survey documentation for a
facility existed and if it was appropriately maintained and tracked in
headquarters and at post. To evaluate the reliability of the data DS uses
to assess risk to office facilities overseas, we examined a copy of the
most recent risk matrix completed by DS[4] and identified (1) inaccurate
information based on post-specific information gathered throughout the
course of the engagement, (2) missing off-compound facilities and
inaccurate information based on an analysis of the facilities included in
the risk matrix, and (3) missing data points. Although we identified data
reliability issues in the risk matrix, which may affect the risk scores for
individual posts, we determined that the data were sufficiently reliable to
broadly characterize overall facility vulnerability and risk scores at the
aggregate level.

To address the adequacy of State's physical security standards, we
evaluated the consistency of select physical security standards across

---

[3]Excess diplomatic work facilities overseas are those the U.S. government owns or leases
but no longer uses.

[4]DS completed the risk matrix we examined in September 2013.

various types of policy guidance and the timeliness of updates to those policies. We conducted a number of activities to evaluate the consistency of physical security standards. We reviewed the physical security standards for work facilities described in the FAM and the FAH—specifically, the FAH sections containing the OSPB standards and the Physical Security Handbook—and identified inconsistencies between the FAM and the FAH and inconsistencies between the two sections of the FAH. We also reviewed policy guidance documented in memoranda and compared that to the physical security standards outlined in the FAH. Finally, we identified inconsistencies between the FAH and the OBO Building and Zoning Codes discussed in an OIG report.[5] To evaluate the timeliness of updates to physical security standards in the FAM and the FAH, we interviewed DS officials to understand the process State follows to update the FAM and the FAH and determined that updates should take approximately 60 to 90 days. We then reviewed (1) all ARB reports resulting from attacks on U.S. diplomatic facilities since 1998 or that included recommendations related to physical security and (2) joint DS-OBO memoranda concerning physical security standards in process. We examined this documentation and identified instances in which it has taken State more than a year to update these standards.

To address how State mitigates vulnerabilities if facilities do not meet applicable physical security standards, we asked post officials a standard set of questions; identified several ways to measure general compliance with physical security standards; and evaluated State's waivers and exceptions process. Using the judgmental sample described above, we traveled to 12 posts and conducted work focused on 4 other posts by teleconference. Our sample included nine countries in three of State's geographic regions—Africa, the Near East, and South and Central Asia. As noted above, we selected these posts due to their relatively high DS-established threat and risk ratings and the presence of facilities that fell within our scope. For security reasons, we are not naming the specific

---

[5]We did not comprehensively review all physical security-related guidance to identify inconsistencies between and within the guidance documents. Rather, we identified the inconsistencies while (1) conducting an analysis of the OSPB standards and the Physical Security Handbook to develop our facility review checklists, (2) reviewing State memoranda concerning physical security requirements, and (3) reviewing a report by the State OIG concerning posts' compliance with security standards. Because it was beyond the scope of this engagement to conduct a systematic review of the consistency of all physical security standards, we cannot generalize our findings to all applicable physical security standards.

posts we visited for this review. At 16 posts overseas, we asked State, USAID, and other agency officials in-person and by video-conference a standard set of questions regarding the implementation of physical security policies and procedures to understand how State identifies and mitigates vulnerabilities.

We also identified three ways to measure general compliance with physical security standards based on State documentation. First, we reviewed the list of embassy and consulate compounds. We found that a significant number were constructed or acquired prior to 1991; because those facilities are only required to meet many of the physical security standards to the maximum extent feasible or practicable, we determined that many of those facilities may not meet standards. Second, we reviewed DS's list of approved waivers and exceptions, which they use to track this documentation, and counted the number of facilities with colocation and setback waivers and exceptions. We determined that each facility with a waiver or exception does not meet all physical security standards. We interviewed DS officials about the waivers and exceptions spreadsheet. While we found problems with some entries in the spreadsheet, we determined that the data were sufficiently reliable to report a general order of magnitude of the number of waivers and exceptions. Third, we obtained and reviewed the 2013 risk matrix that DS completed in September 2013. We then reviewed the facility compliance scores for each facility ranked in DS's risk matrix to determine the number of facilities that DS has found do not meet most OSPB standards for new facilities. To make that determination, we identified all facilities with a standards compliance score in the bottom half of the 10-point range. However, because SECCA's 100-foot setback requirement received its own rating in the matrix and was not considered as part of the facility compliance rating, our analysis of DS's standards compliance score does not include the extent to which facilities met the 100-foot setback requirement. Due to the limitations with DS's ratings that we noted earlier, we are only reporting this information to provide a broad indication of concerns with facilities' compliance with standards and not to provide a precise estimate of the number of facilities with particular ratings.

Furthermore, at 10 posts we visited, we evaluated the compliance of all work facilities—a combined total of 43 different offices and warehouses—against the existing physical security standards. Prior to reviewing overseas facilities, we reviewed prior recommendations made by OIG or the Interagency Security Assessment Teams. We then developed a physical security checklist for each of the four facility types we reviewed—chanceries or consulates, sole occupant of building or compound, tenant

of commercial office space, and unclassified warehouse—on the basis of
the current security standards specified in the OSPB standards and the
Physical Security Handbook. The physical security requirements in the
OSPB standards vary by facility type, date of construction or acquisition,
and threat level. Because we identified some inconsistencies between
these two policy guides, we always included the higher of the two
standards in our physical security checklist in those instances in which we
identified an inconsistency. For example, the OSPB did not include the
compound emergency sanctuary requirement in the OSPB standards until
after our post visits in December 2013. However, because State included
the standards for compound emergency sanctuaries in the Physical
Security Handbook in October 2012, we assessed facilities against this
standard during our facility reviews. We then used these checklists to
evaluate the compliance of work facilities at the 10 posts we visited. In
general, the facilities in our sample were not comparable to those on
recently constructed embassy or consulate compounds, which were
constructed to meet current security standards. Our findings from these
posts are not generalizable to all posts.

To evaluate the adequacy of State's waivers and exceptions process,
which is one process by which State mitigates vulnerabilities when
facilities do not meet standards, we reviewed DS's list of waivers and
exceptions, post-specific physical security surveys, waivers and
exceptions for 14 of the 16 posts in which we conducted work, and our
post-specific physical security checklists for the 10 posts to which we
traveled. We then analyzed DS's list of waivers and exceptions against
the other documentation we collected and our physical security checklists
to identify any issues with DS's tracking of waivers and exceptions. We
also reviewed our physical security checklists and identified all security
deficiencies for which a waiver or exception should have been requested;
we then compared that information with DS's list of waivers and
exceptions and the post-specific waivers and exceptions to identify
missing waivers and exceptions. In addition, we reviewed the post-
specific documentation to determine if post officials requested waivers
and exceptions in a timely manner and if the documentation was
accurate. Finally, we identified mitigation measures outlined in the
approved waiver or exception request that the post was expected to
implement and evaluated that information against our physical security
checklists to determine if all agreed upon mitigation measures had been
implemented.

To address how State's risk management activities align with its policies
and best practices, we assessed DS's risk management policy and,

drawing on our other findings, State's current risk management efforts
against best practices identified by GAO as well as federal standards for
internal control.[6] In addition, we reviewed M/PRI's ARB recommendation
matrix to assess the extent to which State had addressed and closed past
ARB recommendations. However, based on the work we conducted when
reviewing the timeliness of updates to physical security standards, we
identified two instances of recommendations that State closed though it
had not completed the actions cited in closing them.

We conducted this performance audit from March 2013 to June 2014 in
accordance with generally accepted government auditing standards.
Those standards require that we plan and perform the audit to obtain
sufficient, appropriate evidence to provide a reasonable basis for our
findings and conclusions based on our audit objectives. We believe that
the evidence obtained provides a reasonable basis for our findings and
conclusions based on our audit objectives.

The original version of this report is a restricted report and was issued on
June 5, 2014, copies of which are available for official use only.[7] This
public version of the original report does not contain certain information
that State regarded as Sensitive but Unclassified and requested that we
remove. We provided State a draft copy of this public report for sensitivity
review, and State agreed that we had appropriately removed all Sensitive
but Unclassified information.

---

[6]GAO, *Risk Management: A GAO Analysts' Guide*, v. 2.2 (Washington, D.C.: July 2005),
and *Standards for Internal Control in the Federal Government*, GAO/AIMD-00-21.3.1
(Washington, D.C.: November 1999).

[7]GAO, *Diplomatic Security: Overseas Facilities May Face Greater Risks Due to Gaps in
Security-Related Activities, Standards, and Policies* (Washington, D.C.: June 5, 2014).

Appendix II: Comments from the Department of State

United States Department of State
Comptroller
P.O. Box 150008
Charleston, SC 29415-5008

MAY 19 2014

Dr. Loren Yager
Managing Director
International Affairs and Trade
Government Accountability Office
441 G Street, N.W.
Washington, D.C. 20548-0001

Dear Dr. Yager:

We appreciate the opportunity to review your draft report, "DIPLOMATIC SECURITY: Overseas Facilities May Face Greater Risks Due to Gaps in Security-Related Activities, Standards, and Policies" GAO Job Code 320966.

The enclosed Department of State comments are provided for incorporation with this letter as an appendix to the final report.

If you have any questions concerning this response, please contact Paul Ginsburg, Policy Analyst, Bureau of Diplomatic Security at (571) 345-2742.

Sincerely,

Christopher H. Flaggs, Acting

Enclosure: as stated.

cc: GAO – Michael Courts
        DS – Greg Starr
        State/OIG – Norman Brown

Department of State Comments on GAO Draft Report

DIPLOMATIC SECURITY: Overseas Facilities May Face Greater Risks Due to Gaps in Security-Related Activities, Standards, and Policies
(GAO -14-380SU, GAO Code 320966)

Thank you for the opportunity to comment on your draft report entitled DIPLOMATIC SECURITY: Diplomatic Security: Overseas Facilities May Face Greater Risks Due to Gaps in Security-Related Activities, Standards, and Policies. The Department of State welcomes this report. The report includes 13 recommendations for State. State concurs with 12 of the 13 recommendations.

First, GAO recommends that the Office of Management Policy, Rightsizing and Innovation (M/PRI), and the Bureaus of Diplomatic Security (DS) and Overseas Buildings Operations (OBO) define the conditions when a warehouse should be categorized as an office facility and meet appropriate physical security standards. In response, State notes that standards already exist and therefore agrees with the recommendation: 12 FAH-6 and 12 FAH-5 security standards currently allow for a warehouse to contain a supervisor desk position and no others. The standards specifically state that if there are any additional desk positions in a warehouse, then office standards must be applied; a compound emergency sanctuary is required for the protection of non-desk warehouse workers. Additionally, 14 FAH-1 H-318.1-2 (Space Allocation) strongly discourages the creation of office space in a general purpose warehouse.

Second, GAO recommends that M/PRI, DS, and OBO harmonize the terminology State uses to categorize facilities in State's physical security standards and property databases. The Department agrees with this recommendation, and notes that definitional issues across different State bureaus are a challenge that the Department has been actively working to correct through its Enterprise Data Quality Initiative. The Bureaus of Administration, Diplomatic Security, Overseas Buildings Operations and the Office of Management Policy, Rightsizing, and Innovation began work on standardizing the Department's data standards for both domestic and overseas facilities in April 2014. This effort encompasses all domestic installations where State personnel work and all overseas facilities where Chief of Mission personnel live and work. The data from our missions abroad encompasses U.S. government-owned office and residential buildings, leased properties, and applicable host government/third-party locations.

2

Third, GAO recommends that OBO establish a routine process for validating the accuracy of the data in OBO's property database. In response, State agrees. OBO currently has two routine processes already in place for validating the accuracy of the data in the Department's property database. The first process is through the Annual Chief of Mission Management Control Statements of Assurance. The Chief of Mission is required to review and certify that Real Property Application (RPA) data submissions to OBO are timely, complete and accurate. The second routine process is through the annual Federal Real Property Profile submission. OBO reviews and verifies the data being submitted to the Office of Management and Budget (OMB) and the General Services Administration (GSA) to ensure it is accurate and complete. Additionally throughout the year, OBO works closely with internal auditors, Area Management Officers, temporary duty (TDY) realty specialists, and Office of the Inspector General (OIG) inspection teams to review and validate the more than 21,000 records in RPA.

Fourth, GAO recommends DS establish a routine process for validating the accuracy of the data in DS' risk matrix. In response, State agrees. DS has adopted a policy for the collection of information about the vulnerability of office facilities, including setback distances and overall building status, in order to periodically update and validate the data required to complete the risk matrix.

Fifth, GAO recommends the Under Secretary for Management (M) identify and eliminate inconsistencies between and within the FAM, FAH, and other guidance concerning physical security. In response, State agrees. Eliminating inconsistency between 12 FAM, 12 FAH-5 and 12 FAH-6, in addition to updating the standards to meet current requirements, has been an ongoing project. Several drafts of the standards have been completed and are in various stages of approval.

Sixth, GAO recommends State develop physical security standards for additional facilities not covered by existing standards. In response, State agrees. An update to 12 FAH-5 is in the clearance process; it specifically defines the requirements for all facilities. However, there are no standards for stand-alone facilities. That situation will be addressed by the standing Overseas Security Policy Board (OSPB) Physical Security Working Group.

Seventh, GAO recommends State clarify existing flexibilities in the FAH to ensure that security and life-safety updates to the OSPB standards and Physical Security Handbook are updated through an expedited review process. In response, State agrees with GAO's recommendation and DS' Policy and Planning Division

3

(DS/MGT/PPD); the executive secretariat of the OSPB has begun sending policies for Department clearance with a 15-day deadline instead of a 30-day deadline. Additionally, the Chairman of the OSPB, Assistant Secretary Gregory B. Starr, reminds DS and OSPB member agencies at each meeting of the imperative to expedite the review and clearance of security standards sent to them. This occurred recently at the March 25, 2014, OSPB Executive Session Meeting. Coupled with the OSPB's renewed focus to expedite the clearance of standards, DS/MGT/PPD redesigned its OSPB security standards tracking system to better capture timelines and due dates and disseminated this new resource at the last Executive Session meeting.

Eighth, GAO recommends State develop a process to routinely review all OSPB standards and the Physical Security Handbook to determine if the standards adequately address evolving threats and risks. In response, State agrees. Four years ago, DS and OBO formally established the Security Standards Committee (SSC) to review, edit, and draft physical and technical security standards that impact overseas facilities. The SSC meets bi-weekly and is staffed by program managers from DS and OBO. Draft standards are cleared by the committee and approved by the Deputy Director of OBO and the Deputy Assistant Secretary for Countermeasures (DS/C). OSPB standards are then brought before the OSPB working groups for review and clearance.

Ninth, GAO recommends State develop a policy for the use of temporary interim facilities that includes definitions for such facilities, time frames for use, and a routine process for reassessing the temporary or interim designation. State began evaluating this issue earlier in 2014 in response to Congressional requests; we are not in a position to agree or disagree with this recommendation at this time, as a working group is currently evaluating this issue. We have a Support Cell mechanism when we establish a new post, as well as a process to evaluate our presence at temporary or interim posts – the new Vital Presence Validation Process. However, we cannot commit to a policy that includes timeframes given that our Top 80 list and facility issues are often in flux and depend on factors beyond our control such as host government cooperation, availability of buildable land, etc.

Tenth, GAO recommends DS automate its documentation of waivers and exceptions, and ensure DS officials in headquarters and at each post have ready access to post's waivers and exceptions documentation. In response, State agrees. Waivers and exceptions are currently documented in an Excel spreadsheet located on a shared computer drive. This document will be made easily accessible to

4

officials at headquarters and at each post. DS plans to automate the waivers and exceptions process in early 2015, making all associated documentation available on-line.

Eleventh, GAO recommends that DS routinely ensure that necessary waivers and exceptions are in place for all work facilities at posts overseas. In response, State agrees. DS currently coordinates with OBO on all new or renewed leases of functional property to ensure that standards are met, or waivers/exceptions obtained, prior to the occupancy of office space in new facilities; for existing facilities, DS relies upon periodic facility survey reports (which were recently modified to specifically address the status of waivers and exceptions), OIG inspections, and other post visits to identify locations that require waivers or exceptions.

Twelfth, GAO recommends that DS develop a process to ensure that mitigating steps agreed to in granting waivers and exceptions have been implemented. In response, State agrees. A technology process will be instituted for routine compliance follow up at specified intervals after waivers and/or exceptions have been granted; this follow-up will ensure any mitigation strategies that may be required as a condition of the waiver or exception have been completed.

Thirteenth, GAO recommends that State develop a risk management policy and procedures for ensuring the physical security of diplomatic facilities, including roles and responsibilities of all stakeholders and a routine feedback process that continually incorporates new information. In response, State agrees. DS will initiate a new risk management policy process involving OBO and other concerned parties. Receiving automated information from physical security surveys sent from post, combined with the DS/OBO weekly risk meetings will be helpful in achieving this objective.

In conclusion, State thanks the GAO for this constructive audit and will promptly implement the above recommendations to better prepare to operate more effectively in the future.

Appendix III: GAO Contact and Staff Acknowledgments

GAO Contact	Michael J. Courts, (202) 512-8980 or courtsm@gao.gov.
Staff Acknowledgments	In addition to the contact named above, Anthony Moran (Assistant Director), Amanda Bartine, Thomas Costa, David Dayton, Etana Finkler, Farhanaz Kermalli, Ann McDonough-Hughes, Brian Tremblay, and Ozzy Trevino made key contributions to this report. John Bauckman, Martin De Alteriis, Mark Dowling, Brandon Hunt, Mary Moutsos, and Ramon Rodriguez provided technical assistance.

GAO's Mission	The Government Accountability Office, the audit, evaluation, and investigative arm of Congress, exists to support Congress in meeting its constitutional responsibilities and to help improve the performance and accountability of the federal government for the American people. GAO examines the use of public funds; evaluates federal programs and policies; and provides analyses, recommendations, and other assistance to help Congress make informed oversight, policy, and funding decisions. GAO's commitment to good government is reflected in its core values of accountability, integrity, and reliability.
Obtaining Copies of GAO Reports and Testimony	The fastest and easiest way to obtain copies of GAO documents at no cost is through GAO's website (http://www.gao.gov). Each weekday afternoon, GAO posts on its website newly released reports, testimony, and correspondence. To have GAO e-mail you a list of newly posted products, go to http://www.gao.gov and select "E-mail Updates."
Order by Phone	The price of each GAO publication reflects GAO's actual cost of production and distribution and depends on the number of pages in the publication and whether the publication is printed in color or black and white. Pricing and ordering information is posted on GAO's website, http://www.gao.gov/ordering.htm.

Place orders by calling (202) 512-6000, toll free (866) 801-7077, or TDD (202) 512-2537.

Orders may be paid for using American Express, Discover Card, MasterCard, Visa, check, or money order. Call for additional information. |
| Connect with GAO | Connect with GAO on Facebook, Flickr, Twitter, and YouTube. Subscribe to our RSS Feeds or E-mail Updates. Listen to our Podcasts. Visit GAO on the web at www.gao.gov. |
| To Report Fraud, Waste, and Abuse in Federal Programs | Contact:

Website: http://www.gao.gov/fraudnet/fraudnet.htm
E-mail: fraudnet@gao.gov
Automated answering system: (800) 424-5454 or (202) 512-7470 |
| Congressional Relations | Katherine Siggerud, Managing Director, siggerudk@gao.gov, (202) 512-4400, U.S. Government Accountability Office, 441 G Street NW, Room 7125, Washington, DC 20548 |
| Public Affairs | Chuck Young, Managing Director, youngc1@gao.gov, (202) 512-4800 U.S. Government Accountability Office, 441 G Street NW, Room 7149 Washington, DC 20548 |